Logic Programming with Prolog

Max Bramer

Logic Programming
with Prolog

Second Edition

Max Bramer
School of Computing
University of Portsmouth
Portsmouth, UK

ISBN 978-1-4471-5486-0   ISBN 978-1-4471-5487-7 (eBook)
DOI 10.1007/978-1-4471-5487-7
Springer London Heidelberg New York Dordrecht

Printed on acid-free paper

Springer is part of Springer Science+Business Media (www.springer.com)

Introduction

Logic Programming is the name given to a distinctive style of programming, very different from that of conventional programming languages such as C++ and Java. Fans of Logic Programming would say that 'different' means clearer, simpler and generally better!

Although there are other Logic Programming languages, by far the most widely used is **Prolog**. The name stands for Programming in Logic. This book teaches the techniques of Logic Programming through the Prolog language. Prolog is based on research by computer scientists in Europe in the 1960s and 1970s, notably at the Universities of Marseilles, London and Edinburgh. The first implementation was at the University of Marseilles in the early 1970s. Further development at the University of Edinburgh led to a *de facto* standard version, now known as Edinburgh Prolog. Prolog has been widely used for developing complex applications, especially in the field of Artificial Intelligence. Although it is a general-purpose language, its main strengths are for symbolic rather than for numerical computation.

The developers of the language were researchers working on automating mathematical theorem proving. This field is often known as *computational logic*. But if you are not a Computer Scientist, a logician or a mathematician do not let this deter you! This book is aimed at the 99.9 % of the population who are none of these. Those who are, already have a number of excellent textbooks from which to choose.

The idea that the methods developed by computational logicians could be used as the basis for a powerful general purpose programming language was revolutionary 30 years ago. Unfortunately most other programming languages have not yet caught up.

The most striking feature of Prolog for the newcomer is how much simpler the programs look than in other languages. Many language designers started out with good intentions but could not resist, or perhaps could not avoid, making their creations over elaborate. In some languages even writing the customary test program to print out the words *Hello World!* to the user's screen is hard work. All the user has to do in Prolog is to enter **write('Hello World!')**.

Traditional programming languages have one feature in common. They all contain a series of instructions that are to be performed ('executed') one after another.

This style of programming is called *procedural*. It corresponds closely to the way computers are generally built. This is a tempting approach that has been used since the 1950s but is ultimately flawed. The way users write programs should depend as little as possible on how the underlying machine was built and as much as possible on what the user is trying to do. In just the same way, the facilities I use when I drive my car should depend as little as possible on how the engine was designed or the carburettor works. I want all that level of detail hidden from me, although in practice I understand that it may not be completely possible to ignore it.

Prolog programs are often described as *declarative*, although they unavoidably also have a procedural element. Programs are based on the techniques developed by logicians to form valid conclusions from available evidence. There are only two components to any program: facts and rules. The Prolog system reads in the program and simply stores it. The user then types in a series of questions, known as *queries*, which the system answers using the facts and rules available to it. This is a simple example, a series of queries and answers about animals. The program consists of just seven lines (blank lines are ignored).

```
dog(fido).
dog(rover).
dog(henry).
cat(felix).
cat(michael).
cat(jane).
animal(X):-dog(X).
```

This program is not too hard to decipher. The first three lines are *facts*, with the obvious interpretation that fido, rover and henry are all dogs. The next three facts say that felix, michael and jane are all cats.

The final line is a *rule* saying that anything (let us call it X) is an animal if it is a dog. Cat lovers may feel that cats can also claim to be called animals, but the program is silent about this.

Having loaded the program, the user is then faced with the two character symbol **?-** which is called the *system prompt*. To check whether fido is a dog all that is necessary is to type the query **dog(fido)** followed by a full stop and press the 'return' key, which indicates to the system that a response is needed. This gives the complete dialogue:

?- dog(fido).
true.

The user can enter a series of queries at the prompt, asking for further information.

?-dog(jane).   [Is jane a dog? No - a cat]
false.

?- animal(fido).   [Is fido an animal?]
true.   [yes - because it is a dog and any dog is an animal]

?- dog(X).   [Is it possible to find anything, let us call it X, that is a dog?]

X = fido;   [All 3 possible answers are provided]
X = rover;
X = henry

?-animal(felix).   [felix is a cat and so does not qualify as an animal, as far as the
                         program is concerned]
false.

Although straightforward, this example shows the two components of any Prolog program, *rules* and *facts*, and also the use of *queries* that make Prolog search through its facts and rules to work out the answer. Determining that fido is an animal involves a very simple form of logical reasoning:

GIVEN THAT
any X is an animal if it is a dog

AND
fido is a dog

DEDUCE
fido must be an animal

This type of reasoning is fundamental to theorem proving in Mathematics and to writing programs in Prolog.

Even very simple queries such as:

?-dog(fido).

can be looked at as asking the Prolog system to prove something, in this case that fido is a dog. In the simplest cases it can do so simply by finding a fact such as **dog(fido)** that it has been given. The system answers '**true**' to indicate that this simple 'theorem' has been proved.

You have now seen all three elements needed for logic programming in Prolog: facts, rules and queries. There are no others. Everything else is built from them.

A word of warning is necessary at this stage. It is easy for the newcomer to get started with Prolog, but do not be fooled by these examples into thinking that Prolog is only capable of handling simple (Mickey Mouse?) problems. By putting these very basic building blocks together Prolog provides a very powerful facility for building programs to solve complex problems, especially ones involving reasoning, but all Prolog programs are simple in form and are soundly based on the mathematical idea of proving results from the facts and rules available.

Prolog has been used for a wide variety of applications. Many of these are in Mathematics and Logic but many are not. Some examples of the second type of application are

- programs for processing a 'natural language' text, to answer questions about its meaning, translate it to another language etc.
- advisory systems for legal applications
- applications for training
- maintaining databases for the Human Genome project
- a personnel system for a multi-national computer company
- automatic story generation
- analysing and measuring 'social networks'
- a software engineering platform for supporting the development of complex software systems
- automatically generating legally correct licences and other documents in multiple languages
- an electronic support system for doctors.

Prolog is also being used as the basis for a standard 'knowledge representation language' for the Semantic Web – the next generation of internet technology.

Prolog is one of the principal languages used by researchers in Artificial Intelligence, with many applications developed in that field, especially in the form of *Expert Systems* – programs that 'reason out' the solution to complex problems using rules.

Many textbooks on Prolog assume that you are an experienced programmer with a strong background in Mathematics, Logic or Artificial Intelligence (preferably all three). This book makes no such assumptions. It starts from scratch and aims to take you to a point where you can write quite powerful programs in the language, often with considerably fewer lines of program 'code' than would be needed in other languages.

You do not need to be an experienced programmer to learn Prolog. Some initial familiarity with basic computing concepts such as program, variable, constant and function would make it easier to achieve, but paradoxically too much experience of writing programs in other languages may make the task harder – it may be necessary to unlearn bad habits of thinking learnt elsewhere.

Some Technical Details

Experienced programmers will search this book in vain for such standard language features as variable declarations, subroutines, methods, for loops, while loops or assignment statements. (If you don't know what these terms mean, don't worry – you will not be needing them.)

On the other hand experienced readers may like to know that Prolog has a straightforward uniform syntax, programs that are equivalent to a database of facts and rules, a built-in theorem prover with automatic backtracking, list processing, recursion and facilities for modifying programs (or databases) at run-time. (You probably will not know what most of these mean either – but you will be using all of them by the end of this book.)

Prolog lends itself to a style of programming making particular use of two powerful techniques: recursion and list processing. In many cases algorithms that would require substantial amounts of coding in other languages can be implemented in a few lines in Prolog.

There are many versions of Prolog available for PC, Macintosh and Unix systems, including versions for Microsoft Windows, to link Prolog to an Oracle relational database and for use with 'object-oriented' program design. These range from commercial systems with many features to public domain and 'freeware' versions. Some of these are listed (in alphabetical order) below, together with web addresses at which more information can be found.

- Amzi! Prolog
  http://www.amzi.com/products/prolog_products.htm
- B-Prolog
  http://www.probp.com/
- Ciao Prolog
  http://clip.dia.fi.upm.es/Software/Ciao/
- GNU Prolog
  http://gnu-prolog.inria.fr/
- Logic Programming Associates Prolog (versions for Windows, DOS and Macintosh)
  http://www.lpa.co.uk
- PD Prolog (a public domain version for MS-DOS only)
  http://www-2.cs.cmu.edu/afs/cs/project/ai-repository/ai/lang/prolog/impl/prolog/pdprolog/0.html
- SICStus Prolog
  http://www.sics.se/isl/sicstuswww/site/index.html
- SWI Prolog (public domain versions for Windows, Linux and Macintosh)
  http://www.swi-prolog.org/
- Turbo Prolog (an old version that only runs in MS-DOS)
  http://www.fraber.de/university/prolog/tprolog.html

- Visual Prolog
  http://www.visual-prolog.com/
- W-Prolog (a Prolog-like language that runs in a web browser)
  http://waitaki.otago.ac.nz/~michael/wp/
- YAP Prolog
  http://www.ncc.up.pt/~vsc/Yap/

The programs in this book are all written using the standard 'Edinburgh syntax' and should run unchanged in virtually any version of Prolog you encounter (unfortunately, finding occasional subtle differences between implementations is one of the occupational hazards of learning any programming language). Features such as graphical interfaces, links to external databases etc. have deliberately not been included, as these generally vary from one implementation to another. All the examples given have been tested using version 6.2.6 of SWI-Prolog, a popular public-domain version of the language which is available on a range of platforms.

This second edition has been expanded by the addition of two further chapters illustrating the use of grammar rules to analyse English sentences and the use of Prolog for Artificial Intelligence applications.

Each chapter has self-assessment exercises to enable you to check your progress. A full glossary of the technical terms used completes the book.

Max Bramer
Emeritus Professor of Information Technology
University of Portsmouth, Portsmouth, UK
October 2013

Contents

Chapter 1
Getting Started

Chapter Aims

After reading this chapter you should be able to:

- Write and load a simple Prolog program
- Enter goals at the Prolog system prompt
- Understand the basic terminology of the Prolog language
- Distinguish between different types of *term* (data objects).

1.1 Starting Prolog

Starting the Prolog system is usually straightforward, but the precise details will vary from one version to another. Consult the documentation if necessary. Starting Prolog will generally produce a number of lines of headings followed by a line containing just

?-

This is the *system prompt*. (In some versions of Prolog a slightly different combination of characters may be used.)

The prompt indicates that the Prolog system is ready for the user to enter a sequence of one or more **goals**, which must be terminated by a full stop, for example:

?- write('Hello World'),nl,write('Welcome to Prolog'),nl.

nl stands for 'start a new line', as will be explained later. Like all other user input, the above line does not have any effect until the 'return' key is pressed.

Doing so produces the output

Hello World
Welcome to Prolog
true.

followed by a further system prompt ?-.

M. Bramer, *Logic Programming with Prolog*, DOI 10.1007/978-1-4471-5487-7_1,
© Springer-Verlag London 2013

In this book a sequence of goals entered by the user will generally be shown preceded by the **?-** prompt. *The prompt must not be typed by the user.* It is generated automatically by the Prolog system to show that it is ready to receive a sequence of goals.

In the above example, the user has entered a sequence of four goals: **write('Hello World')**, **nl** (twice) and **write('Welcome to Prolog')**. The commas separating the goals signify 'and'.

In order for the sequence of goals

write('Hello World'),nl,write('Welcome to Prolog'),nl

to succeed each of the following goals has to succeed in order:

write('Hello World')

Hello World has to be displayed on the user's screen

nl

a new line has to be output to the user's screen

write('Welcome to Prolog')

Welcome to Prolog has to be displayed on the user's screen

nl

A new line has to be output to the user's screen.

The Prolog system can achieve all these goals simply by outputting lines of text to the user's screen. It does so and then outputs **true** to indicate that the sequence of goals has succeeded.

From the system's point of view, the important issue is whether or not the sequence of goals entered by the user succeeds. The generation of output to the screen is considered much less important and is described as (merely) a *side effect* of evaluating the goals **write('Hello World')** etc.

The meanings of **write** and **nl** are pre-defined by the Prolog system. They are known as *built-in predicates,* sometimes abbreviated to *BIPs.*

Two other built-in predicates that are provided as standard in almost all versions of Prolog are **halt** and **statistics.**

?-halt.

causes the Prolog system to terminate.

?- statistics.

causes system statistics (of value mainly to more experienced users) such as the following to be generated.

0.250 seconds cpu time for 61,957 inferences
4,179 atoms, 2,858 functors, 1,936 predicates, 36 modules, 62,926 VM-codes

1 garbage collections gained 14,448 bytes in 0.000 seconds.
Stack shifts: 2 local, 1 global, 1 trail in -0.000 seconds.
true.

Note that this output ends with the word **true,** signifying that the goal has succeeded, as **statistics, halt** and many other built-in predicates always do. Their value lies in the side effects (generating statistics etc.) produced when they are evaluated.

A sequence of one or more goals entered by the user at the prompt is often called a *query*. We will generally use the term 'sequence of goals' in this book.

1.2 Prolog Programs

Entering a goal or a sequence of goals at the system prompt using only built-in predicates would be of little value in itself. The normal way of working is for the user to load a program written in the Prolog language and then enter a sequence of one or more goals at the prompt, or possibly several sequences in succession, to make use of the information that has been loaded into the database.

The simplest (and most usual) way to create a Prolog program is to type it into a text editor and save it as a text file, say *prog1.pl*.

This is a simple example of a Prolog program. It has three components, known as *clauses*, each terminated by a full stop. Note the use of blank lines to improve readability – they are ignored.

```
dog(fido).
cat(felix).
animal(X):-dog(X).
```

The program can then be loaded for use by the Prolog system using the built-in predicate **consult.**

?-consult('prog1.pl').

Provided that the file *prog1.pl* exists and the program is syntactically correct, i.e. contains valid clauses, the goal will succeed and as a side effect produce one or more lines of output to confirm that the program has been read correctly, e.g.

?-

% prog1.pl compiled 0.02 sec.
true.
?-

> If the Prolog system has a graphical user interface, there will probably be a 'Load' or 'Consult' option provided on a menu as an alternative to using the **consult** predicate. These and other menu options such as 'Exit' are not a standard part of the Prolog language and will not be described in this book.

Loading a program simply causes the clauses to be placed in a storage area called the *Prolog database*. Entering a sequence of one or more goals in response to the system prompt causes Prolog to search for and use the clauses necessary to evaluate the goal(s). Once placed in the database the clauses generally remain there until the user exits from the Prolog system and so can be used to evaluate further goals entered by the user.

Terminology

In the program above the three lines:

```
dog(fido).
cat(felix).
animal(X):-dog(X).
```

are all *clauses*. Each clause is terminated by a full stop. Apart from comments and blank lines, Prolog programs consist only of a sequence of clauses. All clauses are either facts or rules.

dog(fido) and **cat(felix)** are examples of *facts*. They can be interpreted in a natural way as meaning 'fido is a dog' and 'felix is a cat'.

dog is called a *predicate*. It has one *argument*, the word **fido** enclosed in ( ). **fido** is called an *atom* (meaning a constant which is not a number).

The final line of the program

```
animal(X):-dog(X).
```

is a *rule*. The **:-** character (colon and hyphen) can be read as 'if'. *X* is called a *variable*. The meaning of a variable used in a rule or fact is described in Chapter 2. In this context *X* represents any value, as long as it is the same value both times. The rule can be read in a natural way as *X is an animal if X is a dog (for any X)*.

From the above clauses it is simple (for humans) to deduce that **fido** is an animal. Prolog can also make such deductions:

?- animal(fido).
true.

However there is no evidence to imply that **felix** is an animal:

?- animal(felix).
false.

More Terminology

We say that a goal *succeeds* or *fails*, or alternatively that it is *satisfied* or *cannot be satisfied*. The term *evaluating a goal* is used to mean determining whether or not it is satisfied. Equivalently, we can say that a goal evaluates to true (i.e. succeeds) or false (i.e. fails). This all fits in well with the everyday definition of a goal as 'something to be achieved'.

Note that sometimes a goal entered by the user can be interpreted as a command, e.g.

?-halt.

At other times it can be regarded as a question, e.g.

?- animal(fido).
true.

Here is another program about animals. This one comprises eight clauses. All text between /* and */ is taken to be a comment and ignored.

```
/* Animals Program 1 */
dog(fido).
cat(mary). dog(rover).
dog(tom). cat(harry).
dog(henry).
cat(bill). cat(steve).
/* Apart from comments and blank lines, which are
ignored, Prolog programs consist of a number of
clauses. A clause is always terminated by a full
stop. It may run over more than one line, or there
may be several on the same line, separated by at
least one space. There are two types of clause:
facts and rules. dog(tom) is an example of a fact */
```

There are four clauses for predicate **dog** and four for predicate **cat.** We say that the program comprises four clauses defining the **dog** predicate and four defining the **cat** predicate.

Assuming that the program has been saved in a text file 'animals1.pl', the output generated by loading the program and entering a sequence of goals at the system prompt is given below.

?-consult('animals1.pl').	System prompt
% animals1.pl compiled 0.00 sec.	animals1.pl loaded using consult
true.	

?-dog(fido).
true.

?-dog(daisy).
false.

?- dog(X).	
X = fido	pauses – user presses return key

?- dog(Y).	
Y = fido ;	pauses – user presses ;
Y = rover ;	pauses – user presses ;
Y = tom ;	pauses – user presses ;
Y = henry	No pause – goes on to next line

?- cat(X).	
X = mary ;	pauses – user presses ;
X = harry	pauses – user presses return

?- listing(dog).	List all the clauses defining predicate dog

dog(fido).
dog(rover).
dog(tom).
dog(henry).
true.
?-

There are several new features of Prolog introduced in this example. The query

?- dog(X).

(a single goal) means 'find a value of *X* for which the goal **dog(X)** is satisfied', or effectively 'find a value of *X* which is the name of a dog'. Prolog answers

X=fido

However there are other possible answers (**rover, tom** and **henry**). Because of this Prolog pauses and waits for the user to press the 'return' key before it outputs the system prompt **?-**.

The next query entered is

?- dog(Y).

This is essentially the same query as before. It is unimportant which variable *(X or Y)* is used. The query means 'find a value of *Y* which is the name of a dog'. Prolog answers

Y = fido

and again pauses. This time the user presses the ; (semicolon) key. Prolog now looks for an alternative solution or, more precisely, an alternative value of *Y* that satisfies the goal **dog(Y).** It replies

Y = rover

It pauses again and the user again presses the **;** key. A further solution is given

Y = tom

Prolog pauses again. The user again presses the **;** key, producing a further solution

Y = henry

This time there are no more solutions available and Prolog recognises this by not pausing, but immediately going on to output the system prompt **?-**.

The process of finding alternative ways of satisfying a goal by entering a semicolon at the system prompt is known as *backtracking*, or more precisely 'forcing the Prolog system to backtrack'. Backtracking will be discussed in more detail in Chapter 3.

The example also introduces a new built-in predicate. Entering the goal

?-listing(dog).

causes Prolog to list all four clauses defining predicate **dog,** in the order in which they were loaded into the database (which is the same as the order in which they appeared in file animals1.pl).

The next example shows more about the use of variables in queries. The sequence of goals

?-cat(X),dog(Y).

gives all possible combinations of a dog and a cat.

?-cat(X),dog(Y).
X = mary ,
Y = fido ;

X = mary ,

Y = **rover** ;

X = **mary** ,
Y = **tom** ;

X = **mary** ,
Y = **henry** ;

etc.

By contrast, the sequence of goals

?-cat(X),dog(X).

gives all animals which are *both* a cat and a dog (there are no such animals in the database). Although *X* stands for 'any value' in both **cat(X)** and **dog(X)** they must both be the *same* value.

?- cat(X),dog(X).
false.

1.3   Data Objects in Prolog: Prolog Terms

The data objects in Prolog are called *terms*. Examples of terms that have been used in Prolog programs so far in this book are **fido, dog(henry), X** and **cat(X).**

There are several different types of term, which are listed below.

(1) **Numbers**

All versions of Prolog allow the use of integers (whole numbers). They are written as any sequence of numerals from 0 to 9, optionally preceded by a + or - sign, for example:

623
-47
+5
025

Most versions of Prolog also allow the use of numbers with decimal points. They are written in the same way as integers, but contain a single decimal point, anywhere except before an optional + or - sign, e.g.

6.43
-.245
+256.

(2) **Atoms**

Atoms are constants that do not have numerical values. There are three ways in which atoms can be written.

(a) Any sequence of one or more letters (upper or lower case), numerals and underscores, beginning with a lower case letter, e.g.

john
today_is_Tuesday
fred_jones
a32_BCD

but not

Today
today-is-Tuesday
32abc

(b) Any sequence of characters enclosed in single quotes, including spaces and upper case letters, e.g.

'Today is Tuesday'
'today-is-Tuesday'
'32abc'

(c) Any sequence of one or more special characters from a list that includes the following + - * / > < = & # @ :

Examples

+++
>=
>
+-

(3) Variables

In a query a variable is a name used to stand for a term that is to be determined, e.g. variable X may stand for atom *dog*, the number 12.3, or a compound term or a list (both to be described below). The meaning of a variable when used in a rule or fact is described in Chapter 2.

The name of a variable is denoted by any sequence of one or more letters (upper or lower case), numerals and underscores, beginning with an upper case letter or underscore, e.g.

X
Author
Person_A
_123A

but not

45_ABC
Person-A
author

Note: The variable _ which consists of just a single underscore is known as *the anonymous variable* and is reserved for a special purpose (see Chapter 2).

(4) Compound Terms

Compound terms are of fundamental importance in writing Prolog programs. A compound term is a structured data type that begins with an atom, known here as a *functor*. The functor is followed by a sequence of one or more *arguments*, which are enclosed in brackets and separated by commas. The general form is

functor($t_1,t_2, \ldots ,t_n$) $n \geq 1$

If you are familiar with other programming languages, you may find it helpful to think of a compound term as representing a record structure. The functor represents the name of the record, while the arguments represent the record fields.

The number of arguments a compound term has is called its *arity*. Some examples of compound terms are:

likes(paul,prolog)
read(X)
dog(henry)
cat(X)
>(3,2)
person('john smith',32,doctor,london)

Each argument of a compound term must be a term, which can be of any kind including a compound term. Thus some more complex examples of compound terms are:

likes(dog(henry),Y)
pred3(alpha,beta,gamma,Q)
pred(A,B,likes(X,Y),-4,pred2(3,pred3(alpha,beta,gamma,Q)))

(5) Lists

A list is often considered to be a special type of compound term, but in this book it will be treated as a separate type of data object.

Lists are written as an unlimited number of arguments (known as *list elements*) enclosed in square brackets and separated by commas, e.g. [dog,cat,fish,man]. Unlike the arity of a compound term, the number of elements a list has does not have to be decided in advance when a program is written, as will be explained in Chapter 9. This can be extremely useful.

At this stage, all that it is necessary to know is that an element of a list may be a term of any kind, including a compound term or another list, e.g.

[dog,cat,y,mypred(A,b,c),[p,q,R],z]
[[john,28],[mary,56,teacher],robert,parent(victoria,albert),[a,b,[c,d,e],f],29]
[[portsmouth,edinburgh,london,dover],[portsmouth,london,edinburgh],[glasgow]]

A list with no elements is known as the *empty list*. It is written as [].

(6) **Other Types of Term**

Some dialects of Prolog allow other types of term, e.g. *character strings*. These will not be described in this book. However, it is possible to use atoms to perform a rudimentary type of string processing (see Chapter 10).

Atoms and compound terms have a special importance in Prolog clauses and are known collectively as *call terms*. We will return to this in future chapters.

Chapter Summary

This chapter shows how to write simple Prolog programs, load them into the Prolog database and enter goals that can be evaluated using them. It also introduces basic terminology and the different types of data object (terms).

Practical Exercise 1

Specimen solutions to all the Practical Exercises are given in Appendix 3.

(1) Create a disk file animals.pl containing Animals Program 1 (leaving out the comments). Start up Prolog and load your program.

Test your program with the queries given in the text and some others of your own.

(2) Write a program to put facts indicating that a lion, a tiger and a cow are animals into the database and to record that two of them (lion and tiger) are carnivores.

Save your program to a disk file and load it. Check that the database is correct using **listing.**

Enter goals to test whether:

(a) there is such an animal as a tiger in the database
(b) a cow and a tiger are both in the database (a conjunction of two goals)
(c) a lion is an animal and also a carnivore
(d) a cow is an animal and also a carnivore.

(3) Try to predict what Prolog will output in response to each of the following goals, and then try them.

```
?-write(hello).
?-write(Hello).
?-write('Hello!').
?-write('Hello!'),nl.
?-100=100.
?-100=1000/10.
?-100 is 1000/10.
?-1000 is 100*10.
?-2 is (5+7)/6.
?-74 is (5+7)*6.
```

Chapter 2
Clauses and Predicates

Chapter Aims

After reading this chapter you should be able to:

- Identify the components of rules and facts
- Explain the meaning of the term predicate
- Make correct use of variables in goals and clauses.

2.1 Clauses

Apart from comments and blank lines, which are ignored, a Prolog program consists of a succession of *clauses*. A clause can run over more than one line or there may be several on the same line. A clause is terminated by a dot character, followed by at least one 'white space' character, e.g. a space or a carriage return.

There are two types of clause: *facts* and *rules*. Facts are of the form

head.

head is called the *head of the clause*. It takes the same form as a goal entered by the user at the prompt, i.e. it must be an atom or a compound term. Atoms and compound terms are known collectively as *call terms*. The significance of call terms will be explained in Chapter 3.

Some examples of facts are:

```
christmas.
likes(john,mary).
likes(X,prolog).
dog(fido).
```

M. Bramer, *Logic Programming with Prolog*, DOI 10.1007/978-1-4471-5487-7_2,
© Springer-Verlag London 2013

Rules are of the form:

head:-t₁,t₂, ... , tₖ. (k>=1)

head is called the *head of the clause* (or the *head of the rule*) and, as for facts, must be a call term, i.e. an atom or a compound term.

:- is called the neck of the clause (or the '*neck operator*'). It is read as 'if'.

$t_1,t_2, \ldots, t_k$ is called the *body of the clause* (or the *body of the rule*). It specifies the conditions that must be met in order for the conclusion, represented by the head, to be satisfied. The body consists of one or more components, separated by commas. The components are *goals* and the commas are read as 'and'.

Each goal must be a call term, i.e. an atom or a compound term. A rule can be read as '*head* is true if $t_1, t_2, \ldots, t_k$ are all true'.

The head of a rule can also be viewed as a *goal* with the components of its body viewed as subgoals. Thus another reading of a rule is 'to achieve goal *head*, it is necessary to achieve subgoals $t_1, t_2, \ldots, t_k$ in turn'.

Some examples of rules are:

```
large_animal(X):-animal(X),large(X).
grandparent(X,Y):-father(X,Z),parent(Z,Y).
go:-write('hello world'),nl.
```

Here is another version of the animals program, which includes both facts and rules.

```
/* Animals Program 2*/
dog(fido). large(fido).
cat(mary). large(mary).
dog(rover). dog(jane).
dog(tom). large(tom). cat(harry).
dog(fred). dog(henry).
cat(bill). cat(steve).
small(henry). large(fred).
large(steve). large(jim).
large(mike).
large_animal(X):- dog(X),large(X).
large_animal(Z):- cat(Z),large(Z).
```

fido, *mary*, *jane* etc. are atoms, i.e. constants, indicated by their initial lower case letters. *X* and *Y* are variables, indicated by their initial capital letters.

The first 18 clauses are facts. The final two clauses are rules.

2.2 Predicates

The following simple program has five clauses. For each of the first three clauses, the head is a compound term with *functor* **parent** and *arity* 2 (i.e. two arguments).

```
parent(victoria,albert).
parent(X,Y):-father(X,Y).
parent(X,Y):-mother(X,Y).
father(john,henry).
mother(jane,henry).
```

It is possible (although likely to cause confusion) for the program also to include clauses for which the head has functor **parent,** but a different arity, for example

```
parent(john).
parent(X):-son(X,Y).
/* X is a parent if X has a son Y */
```

It is also possible for **parent** to be used as an atom in the same program, for example in the fact

```
animal(parent).
```

but this too is likely to cause confusion.

All the clauses (facts and rules) for which the head has a given combination of functor and arity comprise a definition of a *predicate*. The clauses do not have to appear as consecutive lines of a program but it makes programs easier to read if they do.

The clauses given above define two predicates with the name **parent,** one with arity two and the other with arity one. These can be written (in textbooks, reference manuals etc., not in programs) as **parent/2** and **parent/1,** to distinguish between them. When there is no risk of ambiguity, it is customary to refer to a predicate as just **dog, large_animal** etc.

Note that a query such as

?-listing(mypred).

gives a listing of all the clauses for predicate **mypred** whatever the arity.

An atom appearing as a fact or as the head of a rule, e.g.

```
christmas.
go:-parent(john,B),
    write('john has a child named '),
    write(B),nl.
```

can be regarded as a predicate with no arguments, e.g. **go/0.**

There are five predicates defined in Animals Program 2: **dog/1, cat/1, large/1, small/1** and **large_animal/1.** The first 18 clauses are facts defining the predicates **dog/1, cat/1, large/1** and **small/1** (6, 4, 7 and 1 clauses, respectively). The final two clauses are rules, which together define the predicate **large_animal/1.**

Declarative and Procedural Interpretations of Rules

Rules have both a *declarative* and a *procedural* interpretation. For example, the declarative interpretation of the rule

```
chases(X,Y):-dog(X),cat(Y),write(X),
    write(' chases '),write(Y),nl.
```

is: **'chases (X,Y)** is true if **dog(X)** is true and **cat(Y)** is true and **write(X)** is true, etc.'

The procedural interpretation is 'To satisfy **chases(X,Y),** first satisfy **dog(X),** then satisfy **cat(Y),** then satisfy **write(X),** etc.'

Facts are generally interpreted *declaratively*, e.g.

```
dog(fido).
```

is read as 'fido is a dog'.

The order of the clauses defining a predicate and the order of the goals in the body of each rule are irrelevant to the declarative interpretation but of vital importance to the procedural interpretation and thus to determining whether or not the sequence of goals entered by the user at the system prompt is satisfied. When evaluating a goal, the clauses in the database are examined from top to bottom. Where necessary, the goals in the body of a rule are examined from left to right. This topic will be discussed in detail in Chapter 3.

A user's program comprises facts and rules that define new predicates. These are called *user-defined predicates*. In addition there are standard predicates predefined by the Prolog system. These are known as *built-in predicates* (BIPs) and may not be redefined by a user program. Some examples are: **write/1, nl/0, repeat/0, member/2, append/3, consult/1, halt/0.** Some BIPs are common to all versions of Prolog. Others are version-dependent.

Two of the most commonly used built-in predicates are **write/1** and **nl/0.**
The **write/1** predicate takes a term as its argument, e.g.

write(hello)
write(X)
write('hello world')

Providing its argument is a valid term, the **write** predicate always succeeds and
as a side effect writes the value of the term to the user's screen. To be more precise
it is output to the *current output stream*, which by default will be assumed to be the
user's screen. Information about output to other devices is given in Chapter 5. If the
argument is a quoted atom, e.g. 'hello world', the quotes are not output.

The **nl/0** predicate is an atom, i.e. a predicate that takes no arguments. The
predicate always succeeds and as a side effect starts a new line on the user's screen.

The name of a user-defined predicate (the functor) can be any atom, with a few
exceptions, except that you may not redefine any of the Prolog system's built-in
predicates. You are most unlikely to want to redefine the **write/1** predicate by putting
a clause such as

```
write(27).
```

or

```
write(X):-dog(X).
```

in your programs, but if you do the system will give an error message such as 'illegal
attempt to redefine a built-in predicate'.

The most important built-in predicates are described in Appendix 1. Each version
of Prolog is likely to have others – sometimes many others – and if you accidentally
use one of the same name and arity for one of your own predicates you will get
an error message such as 'illegal attempt to redefine a built-in predicate' or 'no
permission to modify procedure', which can be very puzzling.

In some versions of Prolog it may be permitted to define a predicate with the
same functor and a different arity, e.g. **write/3** but this is definitely best avoided.

Simplifying Entry of Goals

In developing or testing programs it can be tedious to enter repeatedly at the system
prompt a lengthy sequence of goals such as

?-dog(X),large(X),write(X),write(' is a large dog'),nl.

A commonly used programming technique is to define a predicate such as **go/0**
or **start/0,** with the above sequence of goals as the right-hand side of a rule, e.g.

```
go:-dog(X),large(X),write(X),
    write(' is a large dog'),nl.
```

This enables goals entered at the prompt to be kept brief, e.g.

?-go.

Recursion

An important technique for defining predicates, which will be used frequently later in this book, is to define them in terms of themselves. This is known as a *recursive definition*. There are two forms of recursion.

(a) Direct recursion. Predicate **pred1** is defined in terms of itself.
(b) Indirect recursion. Predicate **pred1** is defined using **pred2,** which is defined using **pred3,** ..., which is defined using **pred1.**

The first form is more common. An example of it is

```
likes(john,X):-likes(X,Y),dog(Y).
```

which can be interpreted as 'john likes anyone who likes at least one dog'.

Predicates and Functions

The use of the term 'predicate' in Prolog is closely related to its use in mathematics. Without going into technical details (this is not a book on mathematics) a predicate can be thought of as a relationship between a number of values (its arguments) such as *likes(henry,mary)* or $X=Y$, which can be either true or false.

This contrasts with a *function*, such as $6+4$, *the square root of* 64 or *the first three characters of* 'hello world', which can evaluate to a number, a string of characters or some other value as well as true and false. Prolog does not make use of functions except in arithmetic expressions (see Chapter 4).

2.3 Loading Clauses

Using the built-in predicate **consult/1** causes the clauses contained in a text file to be loaded into the database as a side effect. A Prolog program is just a collection of clauses (rules and facts) so we will refer to a file used this way as a *program file*.

A common method of program development is to load an entire program (set of clauses) as a single file, test it, then make changes, save the changes in a new version of the file, consult the file again to load the clauses from the new version of the file, and so on until a 'perfect' version of the program is achieved.

We will show how repeated use of **consult/1** in this way works using a file that contains only facts (not rules) in the interest of simplicity.

Say that file *testfile.pl* contains the lines

```
alpha.
beta.

dog(fido).
dog(misty).
dog(harry).

cat(jane).
cat(mary).
```

then the query

?-consult('testfile.pl').

puts all seven of the above clauses into the database.

If we now change file *testfile.pl* to

```
gamma.

dog(patch).

elephant(dumbo).
elephant(fred).
```

then after a further

?-consult('testfile.pl').

query the database contains the clauses

```
gamma.

dog(patch).

elephant(dumbo).
elephant(fred).
```

All the clauses placed in the database by the first **consult** have been removed and have been replaced by the contents of the second version of *testfile.pl*. The two **cat** clauses are amongst those removed, which may not have been the user's intention.

Consulting a file is done so often that there is a simplified notation available for it.

?-['testfile.pl'].

is equivalent to

?-consult('testfile.pl').

Filenames are considered to be relative to the directory from which Prolog started up. To consult a file in another directory, the usual file naming conventions are available, e.g.

?-consult('/mydir/testfile.pl').

or

?-['../../mydir/testfile.pl'].

Windows used are advised that the usual backslash character in file names should be replaced by a forward slash.

It is sometimes preferable to break a program (set of clauses) into several files and load them separately. The next example shows the effect of consulting files with different names.

Suppose that the first and second versions of *testfile.pl* above are placed in two files with different names, so that file *testfile1.pl* contains the lines

```
alpha.
beta.

dog(fido).
dog(misty).
dog(harry).

cat(jane).
cat(mary).
```

and testfile2. pl contains the lines

```
gamma.

dog(patch).

elephant(dumbo).
elephant(fred).
```

then the query

?-consult('testfile1.pl'), consult('testfile2.pl').

places the following clauses in the database

```
gamma.
alpha.
beta.

dog(patch).

cat(jane).
cat(mary).

elephant(dumbo).
elephant(fred).
```

We can see that

* The atom *gamma* from *testfile2.pl* has been added to the database to join the two atoms already there from *testfile1.pl*.
* The two clauses for **cat/1** loaded from *testfile1.pl* remain in the database.
* The two clauses for **elephant/1** have been loaded into the database from *testfile2.pl*.
* In the case of the **dog/1** predicate, for which there are clauses in both files, the effect of consulting them in the order given is that the three **dog/1** clauses in *testfile1.pl* have been deleted and replaced by the single **dog/1** clause in *testfile2.pl*.

The last of these may well not be what was intended. It also means that the queries

?-consult('testfile1.pl'), consult('testfile2.pl').

and

?-consult('testfile2.pl'), consult('testfile1.pl').

would give different results as far as the **dog/1** predicate is concerned. It seems a good practical policy when using multiple files to keep the predicates in them separate.

The simplified notation can also be used when consulting multiple files, so for example

?-['myfilea.pl', 'myfileb.pl', 'myfilec.pl'].

has the same effect as

?-consult('myfilea.pl'), consult('myfileb.pl'),consult('myfilec.pl').

2.4   Variables

Variables can be used in the head or body of a clause and in goals entered at the system prompt. However, their interpretation depends on where they are used.

Variables in Goals

Variables in goals can be interpreted as meaning 'find values of the variables that make the goal satisfied'. For example, the goal

?-large_animal(A).

can be read as 'find a value of A such that **large_animal(A)** is satisfied'.

A third version of the Animals Program is given below (only the clauses additional to those in Animals Program 2 in Section 2.1 are shown).

```
/* Animals Program 3 */
/* As Animals Program 2 but with the additional
rules given below */
chases(X,Y):-
  dog(X),cat(Y),
  write(X),write(' chases '),write(Y),nl.
/* chases is a predicate with two arguments*/
go:-chases(A,B).
/* go is a predicate with no arguments */
```

A goal such as

?-chases(X,Y).

means find values of variables *X* and *Y* to satisfy **chases(X,Y).**

To do this, Prolog searches through all the clauses defining the predicate **chases** (there is only one in this case) from top to bottom until a matching clause is found. It then works through the goals in the body of that clause one by one, working from left to right, attempting to satisfy each one in turn. This process is described in more detail in Chapter 3.

The output produced by loading Animals Program 3 and entering some typical goals at the prompt is as follows.

?-consult('animals3.pl').   *System prompt*
% animals3.pl compiled 0.02 sec.   *animals3.pl loaded*

?- chases(X,Y).   User backtracks to find first two solutions only.
fido chases mary
X = fido ,

Y = mary ;   Note use of *write* and *nl* predicates

fido chases harry
X = fido ,
Y = harry
?-chases(D,henry).   Nothing chases henry
false.

?-go.   Note that no variable values are output. (The output is from the *write*
                                  and *nl* predicates, followed by the word 'true'.) In some versions of
                                  Prolog, the user is given the opportunity to backtrack, as here. In
                                  others they are not.
fido chases mary
true;
fido chases harry
true;
fido chases bill
true

It should be noted that there is nothing to prevent the same answer being generated more than once by backtracking. For example if the program is

```
chases(fido,mary):-fchasesm.
chases(fido,john).
chases(fido,mary):-freallychasesm.
fchasesm.
freallychasesm.
```

The query **?-chases(fido,X)** will produce two identical answers out of three by backtracking.

?- chases(fido,X).
X = mary ;
X = john ;
X = mary
?-

Binding Variables

Initially all variables used in a clause are said to be *unbound,* meaning that they do not have values. When the Prolog system evaluates a goal some variables may be given values such as *dog,* -6.4 etc. This is known as *binding* the variables. A variable that has been bound may become unbound again and possibly then bound to a different value by the process of *backtracking,* which will be described in Chapter 3.

Lexical Scope of Variables

In a clause such as

```
parent(X,Y):-father(X,Y).
```

the variables *X* and *Y* are entirely unrelated to any other variables with the same name used elsewhere. All occurrences of variables *X* and *Y* in the clause can be replaced consistently by any other variables, e.g. by *First_person* and *Second_person* giving

```
parent(First_person,Second_person):-
  father(First_person,Second_person).
```

This does not change the meaning of the clause (or the user's program) in any way. This is often expressed by saying that the *lexical scope* of a variable is the clause in which it appears.

Universally Quantified Variables

If a variable appears in the head of a rule or fact it is taken to indicate that the rule or fact *applies for all possible values of the variable.* For example, the rule

```
large_animal(X):-dog(X),large(X).
```

can be read as 'for all values of X, X is a large animal if X is a dog and X is large'.
Variable X is said to be *universally quantified.*

Existentially Quantified Variables

Suppose now that the database contains the following clauses:

```
person(frances,wilson,female,28,architect).
person(fred,jones,male,62,doctor).
person(paul,smith,male,45,plumber).
person(martin,williams,male,23,chemist).
person(mary,jones,female,24,programmer).
person(martin,johnson,male,47,solicitor).
man(A):-person(A,B,male,C,D).
```

The first six clauses (all facts) comprise the definition of predicate **person/5,** which has five arguments with obvious interpretations, i.e. the forename, surname, sex, age and occupation of the person represented by the corresponding fact.

The last clause is a rule, defined using the **person** predicate, which also has a natural interpretation, i.e. 'for all *A*, *A* is a man if *A* is a person whose sex is male'. As explained previously, the variable *A* in the head of the clause (representing forename in this case) stands for 'for all *A*' and is said to be *universally quantified.*

What about variables *B, C* and *D*? It would be a very bad idea for them to be taken to mean 'for all values of B, *C* and *D*'. In order to show that, say, *paul* is a man, there would then need to be **person** clauses with the forename *paul* for all possible surnames, ages and occupations, which is clearly not a reasonable requirement. A far more helpful interpretation would be to take variable *B* to mean 'for at least one value of *B*' and similarly for variables *C* and *D*.

This is the convention used by the Prolog system. Thus the final clause in the database means 'for all *A*, *A* is a man if there a person with forename A, surname *B*, sex male, age *C* and occupation *D,* for at least one value of *B, C* and *D*'.

By virtue of the third **person** clause, *paul* qualifies as a man, with values *smith, 45* and *plumber* for variables B, *C* and *D* respectively.

?- man(paul).
true.

The key distinction between variable *A* and variables *B, C* and *D* in the definition of predicate **man** is that *B, C* and *D* do not appear in the head of the clause.

The convention used by Prolog is that if a variable, say *Y*, appears in the body of a clause but not in its head it is taken to mean 'there is (or there exists) at least one value of *Y*'. Such variables are said to be *existentially quantified.* Thus the rule

```
dogowner(X):-dog(Y),owns(X,Y).
```

can be interpreted as meaning 'for all values of X, X is a dog owner if there is some Y such that Y is a dog and X owns Y'.

The Anonymous Variable

In order to find whether there is a clause corresponding to anyone called *paul* in the database, it is only necessary to enter a goal such as:

?- person(paul,Surname,Sex,Age,Occupation).

at the prompt. Prolog replies as follows:

Surname = smith ,
Sex = male ,
Age = 45 ,
Occupation = plumber

In many cases it may be that knowing the values of some or all of the last four variables is of no importance. If it is only important to establish whether there is someone with forename *paul* in the database an easier way is to use the goal:

?- person(paul,_,_,_,_).
true.

The underscore character _ denotes a special variable, called the *anonymous variable*. This is used when the user does not care about the value of the variable.

If only the surname of any people named *paul* is of interest, this can be found by making the other three variables anonymous in a goal, e.g.

?- person(paul,Surname,_,_,_).
Surname = smith

Similarly, if only the ages of all the people named *martin* in the database are of interest, it would be simplest to enter the goal:

?- person(martin,_,_,Age,_).

This will give two answers by backtracking.

Age = 23;
Age = 47

The three anonymous variables are not bound, i.e. given values, as would normally be expected.

Note that there is no assumption that all the anonymous variables have the same value (in the above examples they do not). Entering the alternative goal

?- person(martin,X,X,Age,X).

with variable *X* instead of underscore each time, would produce the answer

false.

as there are no clauses with first argument *martin* where the second, third and fifth arguments are identical.

Chapter Summary

This chapter introduces the two types of Prolog clause, namely facts and rules and their components. It also introduces the concept of a predicate and describes different features of variables.

Practical Exercise 2

(1) Type the following program into a file and load it into Prolog.

```
/* Animals Database */
animal(mammal,tiger,carnivore,stripes).
animal(mammal,hyena,carnivore,ugly).
animal(mammal,lion,carnivore,mane).
animal(mammal,zebra,herbivore,stripes).
animal(bird,eagle,carnivore,large).
animal(bird,sparrow,scavenger,small).
animal(reptile,snake,carnivore,long).
animal(reptile,lizard,scavenger,small).
```

Devise and test goals to find (a) all the mammals, (b) all the carnivores that are mammals, (c) all the mammals with stripes, (d) whether there is a reptile that has a mane.

(2) Type the following program into a file

```
/* Dating Agency Database */
person(bill,male).
person(george,male).
person(alfred,male).
person(carol,female).
person(margaret,female).
person(jane,female).
```

Extend the program with a rule that defines a predicate **couple** with two arguments, the first being the name of a man and the second the name of a woman. Load your revised program into Prolog and test it.

Chapter 3
Satisfying Goals

Chapter Aims

After reading this chapter you should be able to:

- Determine whether two call terms *unify* and thus whether a goal can be matched with a clause in the database
- Understand how Prolog uses unification and backtracking to evaluate a sequence of goals entered by the user.

3.1 Introduction

We can now look more closely at how Prolog satisfies goals. A general understanding of this is essential for any non-trivial use of the language. A good understanding can often enable the user to write powerful programs in a very compact way, frequently using just a few clauses.

The process begins when the user enters a sequence of goals at the system prompt, for example

?- owns(X,Y),dog(Y),write(X),nl.

The Prolog system attempts to satisfy each goal in turn, working from left to right. When the goal involves variables, e.g. **owns(X,Y),** this generally involves binding them to values, e.g. X to **john** and Y to **fido.** If all the goals succeed in turn, the whole sequence of goals succeeds. The system will output the values of all the variables that are used in the sequence of goals and any other text output as a side effect by goals such as **write(X)** and **nl.**

?- owns(X,Y),dog(Y),write(X),nl.
john
X = john,
Y = fido

M. Bramer, *Logic Programming with Prolog*, DOI 10.1007/978-1-4471-5487-7_3,
© Springer-Verlag London 2013

If it is not possible to satisfy all the goals (simultaneously), the sequence of goals will fail.

?- owns(X,Y),dog(Y),write(X),nl.
false.

We will defer until Section 3.4 the issue of precisely what Prolog does if, say, the first goal succeeds and the second fails.

Call Terms

Every goal must be a Prolog term, as defined in Chapter 1, but not any kind of term. It may only be an atom or a compound term, not a number, variable, list or any other type of term provided by some particular implementation of Prolog. This restricted type of term is called a *call term*. Heads of clauses and goals in the bodies of rules must also be call terms. The need for all three to take the same (restricted) form is essential for what follows.

Every goal such as **write('Hello World'), nl, dog(X)** and **go** has a corresponding *predicate*, in this case **write/1, nl/0, dog/1** and **go/0** respectively. The name of the predicate (**write, nl** etc.) is called the *functor*. The number of arguments it has is called the *arity*.

Goals relating to built-in predicates are evaluated in a way pre-defined by the Prolog system, as was discussed for **write/1** and **nl/0** in Chapter 2. Goals relating to user-defined predicates are evaluated by examining the database of rules and facts loaded by the user.

Prolog attempts to satisfy a goal by matching it with the heads of clauses in the database, working from top to bottom.

For example, the goal

?-dog(X).

might be matched with the fact

```
dog(fido).
```

to give the output

X=fido

A fundamental principle of evaluating user-defined goals in Prolog is that any goal that cannot be satisfied using the facts and rules in the database *fails*. There is no intermediate position, such as 'unknown' or 'not proven'. This is equivalent to making a very strong assumption about the database called the *closed world assumption*: any conclusion that cannot be proved to follow from the facts and rules in the database is false. There is no other information.

3.2 Unification

Given a goal to evaluate, Prolog works through the clauses in the database trying to match the goal with each clause in turn, working from top to bottom until a match is found. If no match is found the goal fails. The action taken if a match is found is described in Section 3.3.

Prolog uses a very general form of matching known as *unification*, which generally involves one or more variables being given values in order to make two call terms identical. This is known as *binding* the variables to values. For example, the terms **dog(X)** and **dog(fido)** can be unified by binding variable X to atom **fido,** i.e. giving X the value **fido.** The terms **owns(john,fido)** and **owns(P,Q)** can be unified by binding variables P and Q to atoms **john** and **fido,** respectively.

Initially all variables are *unbound*, i.e. do not have any value. Unlike for most other programming languages, once a variable has been bound it can be made unbound again and then perhaps be bound to a new value by *backtracking*, which will be explained in Section 3.4.

The process of unifying a goal with the head of a clause is explained first. After that unification will be used to explain how Prolog satisfies goals.

Warning: A Note on Terminology

The words unified, unify etc. are used in two different ways, which can sometimes cause confusion.

When we say that 'two call terms are unified' we strictly mean that an attempt is made to make the call terms identical (which generally involves binding variables to values). This attempt may succeed or fail.

For example, the call terms **likes(X,mary)** and **likes(john,Y)** can be made identical by binding variable X to atom **john** and variable Y to atom **mary.** In this case we say that *the unification succeeds*. However there is no way of binding variables to values that will make the call terms **likes(X,mary)** and **dog(Z)** identical. In this case we say that *the unification fails* or that *the call terms fail to unify*.

Expressions such as 'the unification of the two call terms succeeds' are often abbreviated to just 'the two call terms are unified' or 'the two call terms unify'. The intended meaning (the attempt or the successful attempt) is usually obvious from the context, but it is a potential trap for the inexperienced!

3.2.1 Unifying Call Terms

The process is summarised in the following flowchart (Figure 3.1).

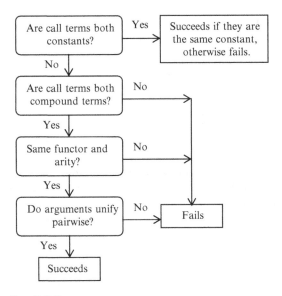

Fig. 3.1 Unifying Two Call Terms

There are three cases to consider. The simplest is when an atom is unified with another atom. This succeeds if and only if the two atoms are the same, so

- unifying atoms **fido** and **fido** succeeds
- unifying atoms **fido** and **'fido'** also succeeds, as the surrounding quotes are not considered part of the atom itself
- unifying atoms **fido** and **rover** fails.

A second possibility is that an atom is unified with a compound term, e.g. **fido** with **likes(john,mary)**. This always fails.

The third and by far the most common case is that two compound terms are unified, e.g. **likes(X,Y)** with **likes(john,mary)** or **dog(X)** with **likes(john,Y)**. Unification fails unless the two compound terms have the same functor and the same arity, i.e. the predicate is the same, so unifying **dog(X)** and **likes(john,Y)** inevitably fails.

Unifying two compound terms with the same functor and arity, e.g. the goal **person(X,Y,Z)** with the head **person(john,smith,27)**, requires the arguments of the head and clause to be unified 'pairwise', working from left to right, i.e. the first arguments of the two compound terms are unified, then their second arguments are unified, and so on. So X is unified with **john,** then Y with **smith,** then Z with 27. If all the pairs of arguments can be unified (as they can in this case) the unification of the two compound terms succeeds. If not, it fails.

The arguments of a compound term can be terms of any kind, i.e. numbers, variables and lists as well as atoms and compound terms. Unifying two terms of this unrestricted kind involves considering more possibilities than unifying two call terms (Figure 3.2).

> ➤ Two atoms unify if and only if they are the same.

> ➤ Two compound terms unify if and only if they have the same functor and the same arity (i.e. the predicate is the same) and their arguments can be unified pairwise, working from left to right.

> ➤ Two numbers unify if and only if they are the same, so 7 unifies with 7, but not with 6.9.

> ➤ Two unbound variables, say *X* and *Y* always unify, with the two variables bound to each other.

> ➤ An unbound variable and a term that is not a variable always unify, with the variable bound to the term.
>   - *X* and **fido** unify, with variable *X* bound to the atom **fido**
>   - *X* and **[a,b,c]** unify, with *X* bound to list **[a,b,c]**
>   - *X* and **mypred(a,b,P,Q,R)** unify, with *X* bound to **mypred(a,b,P,Q,R)**

> ➤ A bound variable is treated as the value to which it is bound.

> ➤ Two lists unify if and only if they have the same number of elements and their elements can be unified pairwise, working from left to right.
>   - **[a,b,c]** can be unified with **[X,Y,c]**, with *X* bound to **a** and *Y* bound to **b**
>   - **[a,b,c]** cannot be unified with **[a,b,d]**
>   - **[a,mypred(X,Y),K]** can be unified with **[P,Z,third]**, with variables *P,Z* and *K* bound to atom **a**, compound term **mypred(X,Y)** and atom **third**, respectively.

> ➤ All other combinations of terms fail to unify.

Fig. 3.2 Unifying Two Terms

Unification is probably easiest to understand if illustrated visually, to show the related pairs of arguments. Some typical unifications are shown below.

person(X,Y,Z)
person(john,smith,27)
Succeeds with variables *X*, *Y* and Z bound to *john*, *smith* and 27, respectively

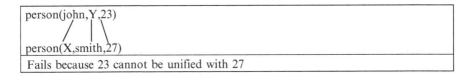

person(john,Y,23)
person(X,smith,27)
Fails because 23 cannot be unified with 27

pred1(X,Y,[a,b,c])
pred1(A,prolog,B)
Succeeds with variables *X* and *A* bound to each other, *Y* bound to atom *prolog* and *B* bound to list *[a,b,c]*

Repeated Variables

A slightly more complicated case arises when a variable appears more than once in a compound term.

pred2(X,X,man)
pred2(london,dog,A)
?

Here the first arguments of the two compound terms are unified successfully, with *X* bound to the atom **london.** All other values of *X* in the first compound term are also bound to the atom **london** and so are effectively replaced by that value before any subsequent unification takes place. When Prolog comes to examine the two second arguments, they are no longer *X* and **dog** but **london** and **dog.** These are different atoms and so fail to unify.

pred2(X,X,man)
pred2(london,dog,A)
Fails because *X* cannot unify with both the atoms *london* and *dog*

In general, after any pair of arguments are unified, all bound variables are replaced by their values.

The next example shows a successful unification involving repeated variables.

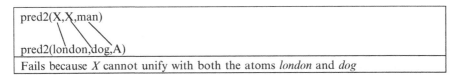

pred3(X,X,man)
pred3(london,london,A)
Succeeds with variables *X* and *A* bound to atoms *london* and *man*, respectively

This example shows a repeated variable in one of the arguments of a compound term.

pred(alpha,beta,mypred(X,X,Y))
pred(P,Q,mypred(no,yes,maybe))
Fails

P successfully unifies with **alpha.** Next *Q* unifies with **beta.** Then Prolog attempts to unify the two third arguments, i.e. **mypred(X,X,Y)** and **mypred(no,yes,maybe).** The first step is to unify variable *X* with the atom **no.** This succeeds with *X* bound to **no.** Next the two second arguments are compared. As *X* is bound to **no,** instead of *X* and **yes** the second arguments are now **no** and **yes,** so the unification fails.

In this example, the second **mypred** argument is now **no** rather than **yes,** so unification succeeds.

pred(alpha,beta,mypred(X,X,Y))
pred(P,Q,mypred(no,no,maybe))
Succeeds with variables *P*, *Q*, *X* and *Y* bound to atoms *alpha*, *beta*, *no* and *maybe*, respectively

3.3 Evaluating Goals

Given a goal such as **go** or **dog(X)** Prolog searches through the database from top to bottom examining those clauses that have heads with the same functor and arity until it finds the first one for which the head unifies with the goal. If there are none the goal fails. If it does make a successful unification, the outcome depends on whether the clause is a rule or a fact.

If the clause is a fact the goal succeeds immediately. If it is a rule, Prolog evaluates the goals in the body of the rule one by one, from left to right. If they all succeed, the original goal succeeds. (The case where they do not all succeed will be covered in Section 3.4.)

We will use the phrase 'a goal *matches* a clause' to mean that it unifies with the head of the clause.

Example

In this example, the goal is

?-pred(london,A).

It is assumed that the first clause in the database with predicate **pred/2** and a head that unifies with this goal is the following rule, which we will call Rule 1 for ease of reference.

```
pred(X,'european capital'):-
    capital(X,Y),european(Y),write(X),nl.
```

The unification binds X to the atom **london** and A to the atom **'european capital'**. The binding of X to **london** affects all occurrences of X in the rule. We can show this diagrammatically as:

```
                              ?-pred(london,A).

pred(london,'european capital'):-capital(london,Y),european(Y),write(london),nl.
X is bound to london, A is bound to 'european capital'.
```

Next Prolog examines the goals in the body of Rule 1 one by one, working from left to right. All of them have to be satisfied in order for the original goal to succeed.

Evaluating each of these goals is carried out in precisely the same way as evaluating the user's original goal. If a goal unifies with the head of a rule, this will involve evaluation of the goals in the body of that rule, and so on.

We will assume that the first clause matched by goal **capital(london,Y)** is the fact **capital(london,england)**. The first goal in the body of Rule 1 is thus satisfied, with Y bound to the atom **england**. This binding affects all occurrences of Y in the body of Rule 1, not just the first one, so we now have

```
                              ?-pred(london,A).

pred(london,'european capital'):-
                  capital(london,england),european(england),write(london),nl.

capital(london,england).
X is bound to london. A is bound to 'european capital'. Y is bound to england.
```

It is now necessary to try to satisfy the second goal in the body of Rule 1, which in rewritten form is **european(england).**

This time we shall assume that the first clause in the database that has a head that unifies with the goal is the rule

```
european(england):-write('God Save the Queen!'),nl.
```

We will call this Rule 2.

Prolog now tries to satisfy the goals in the body of Rule 2: **write('God Save the Queen!')** and **nl**. It does this successfully, in the process outputting the line of text

God Save the Queen!

as a side effect.

The first two goals in the body of Rule 1 have now been satisfied. There are two more goals, which in rewritten form are **write(london)** and **nl.** Both of these succeed, in the process outputting the line of text

london

as a side effect.

All the goals in the body of Rule 1 have now succeeded, so the goal that forms its head succeeds, i.e. **pred(london,'european capital')**.

This in turn means that the original goal entered by the user

?-pred(london,A).

succeeds, with *A* bound to **'european capital'**.

The output produced by the Prolog system would be:

?- pred(london,A).
God Save the Queen!
london
A = 'european capital'

We can now see why output from **write/1** and **nl/0** goals is referred to by the slightly dismissive term 'side effect'. The principal focus of the Prolog system is the evaluation of goals (either entered by the user or in the bodies of rules), by unification with the heads of clauses. Everything else is incidental. Of course, it is frequently the side effects that are of most interest to the user.

This process of satisfying the user's goal creates linkages between the goal, the heads of clauses and the goals in the bodies of rules. Although the process is lengthy to describe, it is usually quite easy to visualise the linkages.

?-pred(london,A).
pred(london,'european capital'):-capital(london,england),european(england),write(london),nl.
capital(london,england).
european(england):-write('God Save the Queen!'),nl.
X is bound to *london*. *A* is bound to *'european capital'*. *Y* is bound to *england*.

Note that the user's goal

?-pred(london,A).

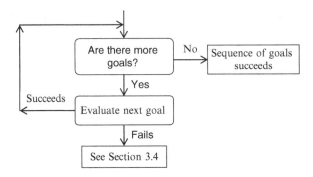

Fig. 3.3 Evaluating a Sequence of Goals

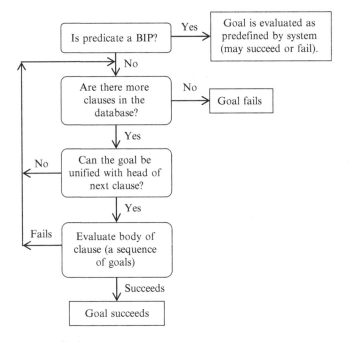

Fig. 3.4 Evaluating a Goal

has been placed to the right in the above diagram. That is because it has much in common with a goal in the body of a rule. A sequence of goals entered by the user at the prompt, for example

?- owns(X,Y),dog(Y),write(X),nl.

is treated in the same way as a sequence of goals in the body of an imaginary rule, say *succeed:-owns(X,Y),dog(Y),write(X),nl.*

The process of evaluating a goal is summarised (in much simplified form) in Figures 3.3 and 3.4. Note that the flowchart for evaluating a sequence of goals refers to the one for evaluating a (single) goal, and vice versa (Figures 3.3 and 3.4).

The principal issue that has been left unconsidered in this account is what happens if evaluation of any of the goals fails. If it does, the Prolog system tries to find another way of satisfying the most recently satisfied previous goal. This is known as *backtracking* and is the topic of the next section. Unification and backtracking together comprise the mechanism that Prolog uses to evaluate all goals, whether entered by the user at the prompt or in the body of a rule.

3.4 Backtracking

Backtracking is the process of going back to a previous goal and trying to *resatisfy* it, i.e. to find another way of satisfying it.

This section gives two very detailed accounts of the way that Prolog tries to satisfy a sequence of goals using unification and backtracking. With practice it is quite easy to work out the sequence of operations by visual inspection of the database. However, it may be helpful to have a detailed account available for reference.

The Family Relationships Example

This example is concerned with family relationships amongst a group of people. The clauses shown below comprise 10 facts defining the **mother/2** predicate, 9 facts defining the **father/2** predicate and 6 clauses defining the **parent/2** predicate.

```
[M1] mother(ann,henry).
[M2] mother(ann,mary).
[M3] mother(jane,mark).
[M4] mother(jane,francis).
[M5] mother(annette,jonathan).
[M6] mother(mary,bill).
[M7] mother(janice,louise).
[M8] mother(lucy,janet).
[M9] mother(louise,caroline).
[M10] mother(louise,martin).
[F1] father(henry,jonathan).
[F2] father(john,mary).
[F3] father(francis,william).
[F4] father(francis,louise).
[F5] father(john,mark).
[F6] father(gavin,lucy).
[F7] father(john,francis).
[F8] father(martin,david).
[F9] father(martin,janet).
```

[P1] parent(victoria,george).
[P2] parent(victoria,edward).
[P3] parent(X,Y):-write('mother?'),nl,mother(X,Y),
      write('mother!'),nl.
[P4] parent(A,B):-write('father?'),nl,father(A,B),
      write('father!'),nl.
[P5] parent(elizabeth,charles).
[P6] parent(elizabeth,andrew).

Facts such as

mother(jane,mark).
father(john,mark).

can be interpreted as meaning 'jane is the mother of mark' and 'john is the father of
mark', respectively.

Note that labels such as [M1] have been added here for reference purposes only.
They are not part of the clauses and must not be included in any program files.
The facts relevant to the following examples can be shown diagrammatically as
follows (with 'f' standing for 'father').

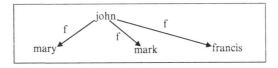

Example 1

Given the query

?-parent(john,Child),write('The child is '),write(Child),nl.

Prolog attempts to satisfy all the goals in the sequence (simultaneously) and in doing
so will find one or more possible values for variable *Child*. It starts with the first goal
parent(john,Child) and attempts to unify it with the head of each of the clauses
defining the predicate **parent/2** in turn, working from top to bottom. It first comes
to clauses [P1] and [P2] but fails to match the goal with (i.e. unify the goal with
the head of) either of them. It next comes to clause [P3] and this time the goal is
successfully unified with the head of the clause, with *X* bound to **john** and variables
Y and *Child* bound to each other.

The system now works through the goals in the body of rule [P3] trying to make
each one succeed in turn. It successfully evaluates the goals **write('mother?')** and
nl, outputting the line of text

?-parent(john,Child),write('The child is'),write(Child),nl.
[P3] parent(john,Y):-write('mother?'),nl,mother(john,Y),write('mother!'),nl.
X is bound to *john*. Variables Y and *Child* are bound to each other.

mother?

as a side effect.

It then comes to the third of the goals, i.e. **mother(john,Y).** This does not unify with the head of any of the clauses [M1] to [M10] which define the **mother/2** predicate, so the goal *fails*.

The system now *backtracks*. It goes back to the most recently satisfied goal in the body of [P3], moving from right to left, which is **nl,** and tries to *resatisfy* it, i.e. to find another way of satisfying it.

Like many (but not all) built-in predicates, **nl/0** is *unresatisfiable*, meaning that it always fails when evaluated during backtracking.

Prolog now moves one further position to the left in the body of [P3], to the goal **write('mother?').** The predicate **write/1** is also unresatisfiable, so this goal also fails.

There are no further goals in the body of rule [P3], working from right to left, so the system rejects rule [P3]. We now have simply

?-parent(john,Child),write('The child is '),write(Child),nl.
Variable *Child* is unbound.

with variable *Child* unbound.

Prolog now goes back to the most recently evaluated previous goal, which in this case is **parent(john,Child),** and tries to resatisfy it. It continues searching through the database for clauses defining the **parent/2** predicate from the point it had previously reached, i.e. clause [P3]. It first examines clause [P4] and successfully unifies the goal with its head, with variable A bound to **john** and variables B and *Child* bound to each other.

?-parent(john,Child),write('The child is '),write(Child),nl.
[P4] parent(john,B):-write('father?'),nl,father(john,B),write('father!'),nl.
A is bound to *john*. Variables B and *Child* are bound to each other.

The system now works through the goals in the body of the rule [P4] trying to make each succeed in turn. The first two goals succeed, with the line of text

father?

output as a side effect.

The system now tries to satisfy the third goal, i.e. **father(john,B)**. It searches through the clauses defining the **father/2** predicate in turn, from top to bottom.

The first clause it matches is [F2], which is a fact. This causes variable B to be bound to atom **mary.** This in turn causes variable *Child* (which is bound to variable B) to be bound to atom **mary.**

?-parent(john,Child),write('The child is '),write(Child),nl.
[P4] parent(john,mary):-write('father?'),nl,father(john,mary),write('father!'),nl.
[F2] father(john,mary).
A is bound to *john.* Variables *B* and *Child* are bound to each other and to atom *mary*

There are two further goals in the body of rule [P4], i.e. **write('father!')** and **nl**. These both succeed with the line of text

father!

output as a side effect. All the goals in the body of [P4] have now succeeded, so the head of the clause, which in rewritten form is **parent(john,mary)**, succeeds. The goal **parent(john,Child)** in the user's query therefore succeeds.

The first of the goals in the sequence entered by the user has now been satisfied. There are three more goals in the sequence: **write('The child is ')**, **write(Child)** and **nl**. They all succeed, as a side effect outputting the line of text

The child is mary

All the goals in the user's query have now been satisfied. The Prolog system outputs the value of all the variables used in the query. In this case, the only one is *Child*.

?- parent(john,Child),write('The child is '),write(Child),nl.
mother?
father?
father!
The child is mary
Child = mary

Forcing the System to Backtrack to Find Further Solutions

The user can now force the system to backtrack to find a further solution or solutions by entering a semicolon character. This works by forcing the most recently satisfied goal, i.e. **nl** (the last goal in the user's query) to fail. The system now backtracks to the previous goal in the sequence, i.e. **write(Child)**. This too fails on backtracking, as does the previous goal, i.e. **write('The child is ')**. The system backtracks a further step, to the first goal in the query, which is **parent(john,Child)**.

The system attempts to find another way of satisfying it, beginning by trying to find another way of satisfying the last goal in the body of [P4]. This is **nl**, which fails on backtracking. So too does the previous goal **write('father!')**.

?-parent(john,Child),write('The child is '),write(Child),nl.
[P4] parent(john,mary):-write('father?'),nl,father(john,mary),write('father!'),nl.
[F2] father(john,mary).
A is bound to *john*. Variables *B* and *Child* are bound to each other and to atom *mary*

It now attempts to resatisfy the previous goal in the body of [P4], working from right to left, which is **father(john,B).** This process begins by rejecting the unification with the head of [F2]. Prolog now continues to search through the clauses defining the **father/2** predicate for further unifications. The next successful unification is with the head of clause [F5]. The terms **father(john,B)** and **father(john,mark)** are unified with variable *B* bound to **mark**. This causes variable *Child* also to be bound to **mark**.

?-parent(john,Child),write('The child is '),write(Child),nl.
[P4] parent(john,mark):-write('father!'),nl,father(john,mark) write('father!'),nl.
[F5] father(john,mark).
A is bound to *john*. Variables *B* and *Child* are bound to each other and to atom *mark*.

This gives a second solution to the user's goal, i.e. a second way of satisfying it. Further backtracking will find a third solution, using clause [F7].

?-parent(john,Child)),write('The child is '),write(Child),nl.
[P4] parent(john,francis):-write('father!'),nl,father(john,francis).
[F7] father(john,francis).
A is bound to *john*. Variables *B* and *Child* are bound to each other and to atom *francis*.

?- parent(john,Child),write('The child is '),write(Child),nl.
mother?
father?
father!
The child is mary

Child = mary ;
father!
The child is mark
Child = mark ;
father!
The child is francis
Child = francis

If the user again enters a semicolon to force the system to backtrack, the system will again go through the backtracking sequence described above, until it reaches the stage of attempting to resatisfy **father(john,B)**, by rejecting the unification with the head of clause [F7] previously found and continuing to search through the clauses defining the **father/2** predicate for further matches. As no further unifications are found, the goal **father(john,B)** in the body of rule [P4] will now fail.

The system now attempts to resatisfy the goal to the left of it in the body of rule [P4]. This is **nl**, which always fails on backtracking. The next goal, again moving to the left, is **write('father?')**, which also fails. There are no further goals in the body of [P4], moving from right to left, so the system rejects rule [P4]. This brings it back to the original goal **parent(john,Child)**, which it tries to resatisfy. It continues to search through the clauses defining the **parent/2** predicate from the point it previously reached ([P4]), but finds no further matches, so the goal fails. As this is the first in the sequence of goals entered by the user, no further backtracking is possible and the user's query finally fails.

?- parent(john,Child),write('The child is '),write(Child),nl.
mother?
father?
father!
The child is mary
Child = mary ;
father!
The child is mark
Child = mark ;
father!
The child is francis
Child = francis
?-

The system prompt is displayed to indicate that there are no more solutions available by backtracking.

Example 2

In the following example the clauses in the database are as before, with the addition of the clauses

> [R1] rich(jane).
> [R2] rich(john).
> [R3] rich(gavin).
> [RF1] rich_father(X,Y):-rich(X),father(X,Y).

Labels such as [R1] have again been added for ease of reference. They are not part of the clauses.

Given the goal

?-rich_father(A,B).

Prolog starts by trying to unify the goal with the heads of all the clauses defining the **rich_father/2** predicate. There is only one, i.e. clause [RF1]. Unification succeeds and variables A and X are bound to each other. Variables B and Y are also bound to each other.

?-rich_father(A,B).
[RF1] rich_father(X,Y):-rich(X),father(X,Y).
Variables A and X are bound to each other. Variables B and Y are bound to each other.

Next Prolog tries to find a value of A satisfying the first goal in the body of rule [RF1]. It does this by searching through the clauses defining the **rich/1** predicate. The first unification it finds is with the head of [R1], i.e. **rich(jane)**. X is bound to **jane**.

?-rich_father(A,B).
[RF1] rich_father(jane,Y):-rich(jane),father(jane,Y).
[R1] rich(jane).
Variables A and X are bound to each other and to atom *jane*. Variables B and Y are bound to each other.

The system now tries to satisfy the goal **father(jane,Y)** by examining the clauses defining the **father/2** predicate, i.e. [F1] to [F9]. None of them unify with the goal, so the system backtracks and attempts to resatisfy (i.e. find another solution to) the most recently satisfied goal, which is **rich(X)**. It continues searching through the clauses defining the **rich/1** predicate, the next unification found being with **rich(john)** (clause [R2]). Now X is bound to **john**, which in turn causes A to be bound to **john**.

?-rich_father(A,B).
[RF1] rich_father(john,Y):-rich(john),father(john,Y).
[R2] rich(john).
Variables A and X are bound to each other and to atom *john*. Variables B and Y are bound to each other.

The system now tries to satisfy the goal **father(john,Y)** by examining the clauses defining the **father/2** predicate, i.e. [F1] to [F9]. The first unification found is with [F2], i.e. **father(john,mary).** *Y* is bound to **mary.**

?-rich_father(A,B).   [RF1] rich_father(john,mary):-rich(john),father(john,mary).   [R2]   rich(john).   [F2] father(john,mary).
Variables *A* and *X* are bound to each other and to atom *john*. Variables *B* and *Y* are bound to each other and to atom *mary*.

There are no more goals in the body of [RF1], so the rule succeeds. This in turn causes the goal **rich_father(A,B)** to succeed, with *A* and *B* bound to **john** and **mary,** respectively.

?- rich_father(A,B).

A = john ,

B = mary

The user can now force the system to backtrack to find further solutions by entering a semicolon character. If so, it attempts to resatisfy the most recently matched goal, i.e. **father(john,Y)** by rejecting the match with [F2] previously found. This causes *B* and *Y* no longer to be bound to **mary** (they are still bound to each other).

The system continues to search the clauses defining the **father/2** predicate for further matches. The next unification found is with the head of clause [F5]. Variable *Y* is bound to **mark.**

?-rich_father(A,B).   [RF1] rich_father(john,mark): -rich(john),father(john,mark).   [R2]   rich(john).   [F5] father(john,mark).
Variables *A* and *X* are bound to each other and to atom *john* . Variables *B* and *Y* are bound to each other and to atom *mark*.

This gives a second solution to the user's goal. If the user forces the system to backtrack again, it will find a third solution using clause [F7] **father(john,francis).**

> ?-rich_father(A,B).
>
> [RF1] rich_father(john,francis):-rich(john),father(john,francis).
>
> [R2]   rich(john).
>
> [F7] father(john,francis).
>
> Variables *A* and *X* are bound to each other and to atom *john*. Variables *B* and *Y* are bound to each other and to atom *francis*.

If the user forces the system to backtrack again, it will start by deeming that the most recently satisfied goal, i.e. **father(john,Y)** has failed. This causes *B* and *Y* no longer to be bound to **francis** (they are still bound to each other).

> ?-rich_father(A,B).
>
> [RF1] rich_father(john,Y):-rich(john),father(john,Y).
>
> [R2]   rich(john).
>
> Variables *A* and *X* are bound to each other and to atom *john*. Variables *B* and *Y* are bound to each other.

The system will fail to find any further matches for the goal **father(john,Y)**. It will next attempt to find further solutions to the most recently satisfied previous goal in [RF1], working from right to left. This is **rich(X)**. This will succeed with *X* now bound to **gavin** (clause [R3]).

> ?-rich_father(A,B).
>
> [RF1] rich_father(gavin,Y):-rich(gavin),father(gavin,Y).
>
> [R3]   rich(gavin).
>
> Variables *A* and *X* are bound to each other and to atom *gavin*. Variables *B* and *Y* are bound to each other.

Working from left to right again, the system will now try to satisfy the goal **father(gavin,Y)**. This will unify with the head of just one of the **father/2** clauses, namely with clause [F6] **father(gavin,lucy)**, with variable *Y* bound to **lucy**.

> ?-rich_father(A,B).
>
> [RF1] rich_father(gavin,lucy):-rich(gavin),father(gavin,lucy).
>
> [R3]   rich(gavin).
>
> [F6] father(gavin,lucy).
>
> Variables *A* and *X* are bound to each other and to atom *gavin*. Variables *B* and *Y* are bound to each other and to atom *lucy*.

All the goals in the body of [RF1] have now succeeded, so the head **rich_father(gavin,lucy)** succeeds, and in turn **rich_father(A,B)** succeeds with *A* and *B* bound to **gavin** and **lucy,** respectively.

Forcing the system to backtrack again will lead to the same sequence of operations as above, right up to the attempt to find further matches for the goal **rich(X)** in the body of [PF1]. This will fail, which will in turn cause [RF1] to fail. This will make the Prolog system go back a further step to try to find another match for the original goal **rich_father(A,B)** with clauses defining the **rich_father/2** predicate. Since there is only one such clause, no more matches will be found and the user's goal will finally fail.

?- rich_father(A,B).
A = john ,
B = mary ;
A = john ,
B = mark ;
A = john ,
B = francis ;
A = gavin ,
B = lucy ;
?-

3.5   Satisfying Goals: A Summary

The method described in the previous sections is shown in diagrammatic form in Figures 3.5 and 3.6. Note how the two flowcharts refer to each other.

Evaluating a Sequence of Goals: Summary

Evaluate the goals in turn, working from left to right. If they all succeed, the whole sequence of goals succeeds. If one fails, go back through the previous goals in the sequence one by one from right to left trying to resatisfy them. If they all fail, the whole sequence fails. As soon as one succeeds, start working through the goals from left to right again.

Evaluating/Re-evaluating a Goal: Summary

Search through the clauses in the database, working from top to bottom[1] until one is found, the head of which matches with the goal. If the matching clause is a fact, the goal succeeds. If it is a rule, evaluate the sequence of goals in its body. If the sequence succeeds, the goal succeeds. If not, continue searching through the database for further matches. If the end of the database is reached, the goal fails.

---

[1] Start at the top (for evaluation) or after the clause matched when the goal was last satisfied (for re-evaluation).

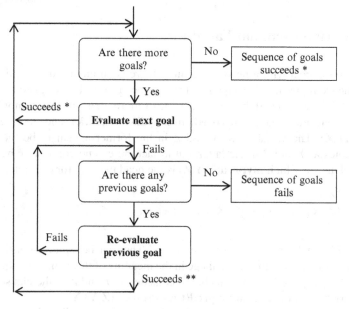

* Some variables may have become bound.
** Some variables may have become bound to other values (or unbound).

Fig. 3.5 Evaluating a Sequence of Goals

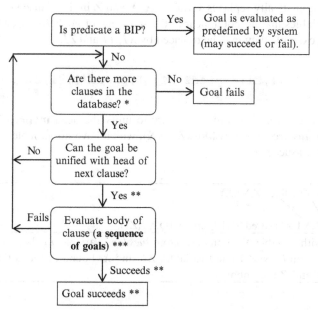

*   Evaluation: Start at top of database.
       Re-evaluation: Start after clause matched when goal last satisfied.
**   Some variables may have become bound.
*** If the clause is a fact there is no body, so the goal succeeds immediately.

Fig. 3.6 Evaluating/Re-evaluating a Goal

3.6   Removing Common Variables

When unifying a goal with a head of a clause, there is an important complication, which all the examples in this chapter so far have been carefully designed to avoid: what happens if the goal and the head have one or more variables in common?

Suppose that the goal is **mypred(tuesday,likes(Z,Y),X)** and the head is **mypred(X,Y,Z)**. The variables *X, Y* and *Z* in the former appear to be the same as the variables *X, Y* and *Z* in the latter, but in fact there is no connection between them. The clause of which **mypred(X,Y,Z)** is the head may be, for example,

```
mypred(X,Y,Z):-pred2(X,Q),pred3(Q,Y,Z).
```

The variables in this rule are just 'placeholders'. They can be replaced consistently by any other variables without any change in the meaning of the clause, as explained in Chapter 2, so it would not be sensible to consider *X, Y* and *Z* in the clause to be the same variables as in the goal **mypred(tuesday,likes(Z,Y),X).**

Before attempting to unify the goal and the head of the clause, it is first necessary to rewrite the clause to ensure that it has no variables in common with the goal. To be precise the clause must not have any variables in common with any of the goals in the sequence of which the goal currently under consideration is part.

Prolog automatically replaces variables *X, Y* and *Z* in the clause systematically by other variables that do not appear in the sequence of goals (or elsewhere in the clause). For example they may be replaced by *X1, Y1* and *Z1*.

```
mypred(X1,Y1,Z1):-pred2(X1,Q),pred3(Q,Y1,Z1).
```

After this rewriting it is only necessary to unify the head **mypred(X1,Y1,Z1)** and the goal **mypred(tuesday,likes(Z,Y),X),** which have no variable in common. The unification succeeds.

| mypred(tuesday,likes(Z,Y),X) |
| mypred(X1,Y1,Z1):-pred2(X1,Q),pred3(Q,Y1,Z1). |
| Succeeds with variable *X1* bound to atom *tuesday* , variable *Y1* bound to compound term *likes(Z,Y)* and variables *Z1* and *X* bound to each other. Variables *Y* and *Z* are unbound. |

3.7 A Note on Declarative Programming

From this chapter it is clear that the order in which the clauses defining a predicate occur in the database and the order of the goals in the body of a rule are of vital importance when evaluating a user's query.

It is part of the philosophy of logic programming that programs should be written to minimize the effect of these two factors as far as possible. Programs that do so are called fully or partly *declarative*.

An example of a fully declarative program is the following, based on Animals Program 2 in Chapter 2.

```
dog(fido). dog(rover). dog(jane). dog(tom). dog(fred).
dog(henry).

cat(bill). cat(steve). cat(mary). cat(harry).

large(rover). large(william). large(martin).
large(tom). large(steve).
large(jim). large(mike).

large_animal(X):- dog(X),large(X).
large_animal(Z):- cat(Z),large(Z).
```

The query

?- large_animal(X).

will produce three possible values of *X* by backtracking

X = rover ;
X = tom ;
X = steve ;
false.

Rearranging the clauses in the program in any order will produce the same three answers but possibly in a different order (try it!).

Rearranging the order of the goals in the bodies of the two rules defining **large_animal/1,** for example to

```
large_animal(X):- large(X),dog(X).
large_animal(Z):- large(Z),cat(Z).
```

will also give the same three answers.

It is often very difficult or impossible to define a predicate in such a way that the order of the goals in the body of each rule is irrelevant, especially when built-in predicates such as **write/1** are involved. However, with a little effort it is frequently possible to write the clauses defining a predicate in such a way that if the order were changed the answers to any query (including those produced by backtracking) would be the same. For example if we wish to test whether a number is positive, negative or zero, we could define a predicate **test/1** like this

```
test(X):-X>0,write(positive),nl.
test(0):-write(zero),nl.
test(X):-write(negative),nl.
```

This relies on the third clause only being reached when the value of X is negative. A more declarative (and better) way of defining **test/1** would be

```
test(X):-X>0,write(positive),nl.
test(0):-write(zero),nl.
test(X):-X<0,write(negative),nl.
```

where the test for X being negative in the third clause is made explicit.

Not only is it considered good Prolog programming style to make programs as declarative as possible, it can greatly reduce the likelihood of making errors that are hard to detect, particularly when backtracking is used. Chapter 7 gives some examples of this.

3.8   Important Note on User-Controlled Backtracking

The use of 'user-controlled' backtracking to find more solutions to a query was illustrated in previous chapters and was explained in detail earlier in this chapter.

The use of backtracking 'behind the scenes' is fundamental to any Prolog system and user-controlled backtracking can certainly be valuable in some situations. However there are other situations where the facility should not be used.

For many of the examples given in this book executing a query produces a solution after which the system pauses to allow the user to attempt to backtrack. In some cases there are no more solutions to be found and if the user enters a semicolon character the system will simply reply

false.

In other cases the system will attempt to find an alternative solution even though no other meaningful solution would be possible, such as finding the larger of two numbers or combining the contents of two text files into a single file. Often the effect of doing so will be to produce output that is 'mysterious' or obviously wrong. In some cases the system will go into an infinite loop and/or crash as the available memory fills up.

The solution to these problems is simply for the user to press the 'return' key to suppress backtracking on all occasions except where there is a good reason to believe that there may be additional solutions available. That is the policy followed in this book, usually without drawing attention to it.

Problems relating to backtracking and how to deal with them will be discussed further in Chapter 7.

Chapter Summary

This chapter demonstrates how Prolog uses unification to match goals with the heads of clauses and how it uses the combination of unification and backtracking to evaluate goals entered by the user and to find multiple solutions if required. The chapter ends with a warning about the use of 'user-controlled' backtracking.

Practical Exercise 3

The program below is a variant of the family relationships program used in Section 3.4. As before, [M1] etc. are labels added to make it easier to refer to the clauses.

```
[M1] mother(ann,henry).
[M2] mother(ann,mary).
[M3] mother(jane,mark).
[M4] mother(jane,francis).
[M5] mother(annette,jonathan).
[M6] mother(mary,bill).
[M7] mother(janice,louise).
[M8] mother(lucy,janet).
[M9] mother(louise,caroline).
[M10] mother(caroline,david).
[M11] mother(caroline,janet).
[F1] father(henry,jonathan).
```

```
[F2] father(john,mary).
[F3] father(francis,william).
[F4] father(francis,louise).
[F5] father(john,mark).
[F6] father(gavin,lucy).
[F7] father(john,francis).
[P1] parent(victoria,george).
[P2] parent(victoria,edward).
[P3] parent(X,Y):-mother(X,Y).
[P4] parent(X,Y):-father(X,Y).
[P5] parent(elizabeth,charles).
[P6] parent(elizabeth,andrew).
[A1] ancestor(X,Y):-parent(X,Y).
[A2] ancestor(X,Y):-parent(X,Z),ancestor(Z,Y).
```

The most important change is the addition of two clauses defining the **ancestor/2**
predicate. Clause [A1] simply states that X is an ancestor of Y if X is a parent of
Y. Clause [A2] is a recursive definition of more distant ancestor relationships which
can be read as 'X is the ancestor of Y if there is some person Z such that X is the
parent of Z and Z is the ancestor of Y'.

(1) Extend the program above by devising rules to define each of the following.
    Load your extended program and test it.

(a) child_of(A,B)
(b) grandfather_of(A,B)
(c) grandmother_of(A,B)
(d) great_grandfather_of(A,B)

(2) Construct a sequence of diagrams similar to those in Section 3.4 to show the
    sequence of events when the Prolog system attempts to satisfy the goal

?-ancestor(louise,Desc).

Find (using backtracking) the first *two* people the Prolog system will identify as
louise's descendants.

Predict the output that will be produced if the user repeatedly forces the system to
backtrack. Verify your prediction by loading the program and testing it.

Chapter 4
Operators and Arithmetic

Chapter Aims

After reading this chapter you should be able to:

- Convert unary and binary predicates to operators
- Evaluate arithmetic expressions and compare their values
- Test for equality of arithmetic expressions and terms
- Use the 'not' and disjunction operators.

4.1 Operators

Up to now, the notation used for predicates in this book is the standard one of a functor followed by a number of arguments in parentheses, e.g. **likes(john,mary).**

As an alternative, any user-defined predicate with two arguments (a *binary predicate*) can be converted to an *infix operator*. This enables the functor (predicate name) to be written between the two arguments with no parentheses, e.g.

john likes mary

Some Prolog users may find this easier to read. Others may prefer the standard notation.

Any user-defined predicate with one argument (a *unary predicate*) can be converted to a *prefix operator*. This enables the functor to be written before the argument with no parentheses, e.g.

isa_dog fred

instead of

isa_dog(fred)

M. Bramer, *Logic Programming with Prolog*, DOI 10.1007/978-1-4471-5487-7_4,
© Springer-Verlag London 2013

Alternatively, a unary predicate can be converted to a *postfix operator*. This enables the functor to be written after the argument, e.g.

fred isa_dog

Operator notation can also be used with rules to aid readability. Some people may find a rule such as

```
likes(john,X):-is_female(X),owns(X,Y),isa_cat(Y).
```

easier to understand if it is written as

```
john likes X:- X is_female, X owns Y, Y isa_cat.
```

The standard bracketed 'functor and arguments' notation, e.g. **likes(john,X)** can still be used with operators if preferred. 'Mixed' notation is also permitted, e.g. if **likes/2, is_female/1, owns/2** and **isa_cat/1** are all operators

```
likes(john,X):-is_female(X),X owns Y,isa_cat(Y).
```

is a valid form of the previous rule.

Any user-defined predicate with one or two arguments can be converted to an operator by entering a goal using the **op/3** predicate at the system prompt. This predicate takes three arguments, for example

```
?-op(150,xfy,likes).
```

The first argument is the 'operator precedence', which is an integer from 0 upwards. The range of numbers used depends on the particular implementation. The lower the number is, the higher the precedence. Operator precedence values are used to determine the order in which operators will be applied when more than one is used in a term. The most important practical use of this is for operators used for arithmetic, as will be explained later. In most other cases it will suffice to use an arbitrary value such as 150.

The second argument should normally be one of the following atoms:

xfx, **xfy** or **yfx** meaning that the predicate is binary and is to be converted to an infix operator

fx or **fy** meaning that the predicate is unary and is to be converted to an prefix operator

xf or **yf** meaning that the predicate is unary and is to be converted to a postfix operator.

(The difference between the alternatives available for each type will be explained in Section 4.5.)

The third argument specifies the name of the predicate that is to be converted to an operator.

A predicate can also be converted to an operator by placing a line such as

?-op(150,xfy,likes).

in a Prolog program file to be loaded using **consult**. *Note that the prompt (the two characters ?-) must be included.* When a goal is used in this way, the entire line is known as a *directive*. In this case, the directive must be placed in the file before the first clause that uses the operator *likes*.

If a program file containing

```
?-op(150,xfy,likes).
?-op(150,xf,is_female).
?-op(150,xf,isa_cat).
?-op(150,xfy,owns).

john likes X:- X is_female, X owns Y, Y isa_cat.

is_female(mary).
owns(mary,fido).
isa_cat(fido).
```

is loaded using **consult** some possible queries are:

?- john likes mary.
true.

?- john likes X.
X = mary.

?- X likes mary.
X = john.

?- X likes Y.
X = john,
Y = mary.

?- is_female(X).
X = mary.

Several built-in predicates have been pre-defined as operators. These include *relational operators* for comparing numerical values, including < denoting 'less than' and > denoting 'greater than'.

Thus the following are valid terms, which may be included in the body of a rule:

X>4
Y<Z
A=B

Bracketed notation may also be used with built-in predicates that are defined as operators, e.g. **>(X,4)** instead of **X>4**.

A list of the principal built-in operators is given in Appendix 2 for ease of reference.

4.2 Arithmetic

Although the examples used in previous chapters of this book are non-numerical (animals which are mammals etc.), Prolog also provides facilities for doing arithmetic using a notation similar to that which will already be familiar to many users from basic algebra.

This is achieved using the built-in predicate **is/2**, which is predefined as an infix operator and thus is written between its two arguments.

The most common way of using **is/2** is where the first argument is an unbound variable. Evaluating the goal **X is −6.5** will cause X to be bound to the number −6.5 and the goal to succeed.

The second argument can be either a number or an arithmetic expression e.g.

X is 6*Y+Z-3.2+P-Q/4 (* denotes multiplication).

Any variables appearing in an arithmetic expression must already be bound (as a result of evaluating a previous goal) and their values must be numerical. Provided they are, the goal will always succeed and the variable that forms the first argument will be bound to the value of the arithmetic expression. If not, an error message will result.

?- X is 10.5+4.7*2.
X = 19.9

?- Y is 10,Z is Y+1.
Y = 10,
Z = 11

Symbols such as + - * / in arithmetic expressions are a special type of infix operator known as *arithmetic operators*. Unlike operators used elsewhere in Prolog they are not predicates but *functions*, which return a numerical value.

As well as numbers, variables and operators, arithmetic expressions can include *arithmetic functions*, written with their arguments in parentheses (i.e. not as operators). Like arithmetic operators these return numerical values, e.g. to find the square root of 36:

?- X is sqrt(36).
X = 6

The arithmetic operator - can be used not only as a binary infix operator to denote the difference of two numerical values, e.g. **X-6,** but also as a unary prefix operator to denote the negative of a numerical value, e.g.

?- X is 10,Y is -X-2.
X = 10,
Y=−12

The table below shows some of the arithmetic operators and arithmetic functions available in Prolog.

X+Y	The sum of X and Y
X-Y	The difference of X and Y
X*Y	The product of X and Y
X/Y	The quotient of X and Y
X//Y	The 'integer quotient' of X and Y (the result is truncated to the nearest integer between it and zero)
X mod Y	The remainder when X is divided by Y
X^Y	The value of X to the power of Y
-X	The negative of X
abs(X)	The absolute value of X
sin(X)	The sine of X (for X measured in radians)
cos(X)	The cosine of X (for X measured in radians)
max(X,Y)	The larger of X and Y
round(X)	The value of X rounded to the nearest integer
sqrt(X)	The square root of X

Example

?- X is 30,Y is 5,Z is X+Y+X*Y.
X = 30,
Y = 5,
Z = 185.

Although the **is** predicate is normally used in the way described here, the first argument can also be a number or a bound variable with a numerical value. In this case, the numerical values of the two arguments are calculated. The goal succeeds if these are equal. If not, it fails.

?- X is 7,X is 6+1.
X = 7

?- **10 is 7+13-11+9.**
false.

?- **18 is 7+13-11+9.**
true.

Unification

The previous description can be simplified by saying that the second argument of the **is/2** operator is evaluated and this value is then *unified* with the first argument. This illustrates the flexibility of the concept of unification.

(a) If the first argument is an unbound variable, it is bound to the value of the second argument (as a side effect) and the **is** goal succeeds.
(b) If the first argument is a number, or a bound variable with a numerical value, it is compared with the value of the second argument. If they are the same, the **is** goal succeeds, otherwise it fails.

If the first argument is an atom, a compound term, a list, or a variable bound to one of these (none of which should happen), the outcome is implementation-dependent. It is likely that an error will occur.

Note that a goal such as **X is X+1** will always fail, whether or not X is bound.

?- **X is 10,X is X+1.**
false.

To increase a value by one requires a different approach.

```
/* Incorrect version */
increase(N):-N is N+1.
```

?- **increase(4).**
false.

```
/*Correct version */
increase(N,M):-M is N+1.
```

?- **increase(4,X).**
X = 5

Operator Precedence in Arithmetic Expressions

When there is more than one operator in an arithmetic expression, e.g. **A+B*C-D**, Prolog needs a means of deciding the order in which the operators will be applied.

For the basic operators such as $+$ $-$ * and / it is highly desirable that this is the customary 'mathematical' order, i.e. the expression **A+B*C-D** should be interpreted as 'calculate the product of B and C, add it to A and then subtract D', not as 'add A and B, then multiply by C and subtract D'. Prolog achieves this by giving each operator a numerical *precedence value*. Operators with relatively high precedence such as * and / are applied before those with lower precedence such as $+$ and -. Operators with the same precedence (e.g. $+$ and -, * and /) are applied from left to right. The effect is to give an expression such as **A+B*C-D** the meaning that a user who is familiar with algebra would expect it to have, i.e. **A+(B*C)-D.**

If a different order of evaluation is required this can be achieved by the use of brackets, e.g. **X is (A+B)*(C-D).** Bracketed expressions are always evaluated first.

Relational Operators

The infix operators =:= =\= > >= < =< are a special type known as *relational operators*. They are used to compare the value of two arithmetic expressions. The goal succeeds if the value of the first expression is equal to, not equal to, greater than, greater than or equal to, less than or less than or equal to the value of the second expression, respectively. Both arguments must be numbers, bound variables or arithmetic expressions (in which any variables are bound to numerical values).

?- 88+15-3=:=110-5*2.
true.

?- 100=\=99.
true.

4.3 Equality Operators

There are three types of relational operator for testing equality and inequality available in Prolog. The first type is used to compare the values of arithmetic expressions. The other two types are used to compare terms.

Arithmetic Expression Equality =:=

E1=:=E2 succeeds if the arithmetic expressions E1 and E2 evaluate to the same value.

?- 6+4=:=6*3-8.
true.

?- sqrt(36)+4=:=5*11-45.
true.

To check whether an integer is odd or even we can use the **checkeven/1** predicate
defined below.

```
checkeven(N):-M is N//2,N=:=2*M.
```

?- checkeven(12).
true.

?- checkeven(23).
false.

?- checkeven(-11).
false.

?- checkeven(-30).
true.

The integer quotient operator **//** divides its first argument by its second and
truncates the result to the nearest integer between it and zero. So **12//2** is 6, **23//2** is
11, **-11//2** is -5 and **-30//2** is -15. Dividing an integer by 2 using **//** and multiplying
it by 2 again will give the original integer if it is even, but not otherwise.

Arithmetic Expression Inequality =\=

E1=\=E2 succeeds if the arithmetic expressions E1 and E2 do not evaluate to the
same value

?- 10=\=8+3.
true.

Terms Identical ==

Both arguments of the infix operator == must be terms. The goal *Term1==Term2*
succeeds if and only if *Term1* is identical to *Term2*. Any variables used in the terms
may or may not already be bound, but no variables are bound as a result of evaluating
the goal.

?- likes(X,prolog)==likes(X,prolog).
true.

?- likes(X,prolog)==likes(Y,prolog).
false.

(X and Y are different variables)

?- X is 10,pred1(X)==pred1(10).

X = 10

?- X==0.
false.

?- 6+4==3+7.
false.

The value of an arithmetic expression is only evaluated when used with the **is/2** operator. Here **6+4** is simply a term with functor **+** and arguments **6** and **4.** This is entirely different from the term **3+7.**

Terms Not Identical \ ==

Term1\==Tem2 tests whether *Term1* is not identical to *Term2*. The goal succeeds if *Term1==Term2* fails. Otherwise it fails.

?- pred1(X)\==pred1(Y).
true.

(The output signifies that both *X* and *Y* are unbound and are different variables.)

Terms Identical With Unification =

The term equality operator = is similar to == with one vital (and often very useful) difference. The goal *Term1=Term2* succeeds if terms *Term1* and *Term2 unify,* i.e. there is some way of binding variables to values which would make the terms identical. If the goal succeeds, such binding actually takes place. Unification is discussed in detail in Chapter 3.

?- pred1(X)=pred1(10).
X = 10

(Variable *X* is bound to 10, which makes the two terms identical.)

?- likes(X,prolog)=likes(john,Y).
X = john ,
Y = prolog

(Binding *X* to the atom *john* and *Y* to the atom *prolog* makes the two terms identical.)

?- X=0,X=:=0.
X = 0

(*X*=0 causes *X* to be bound to 0. The goal **X=:=0** succeeds, which confirms that *X* now has the value zero.)

?- 6+4=3+7.
false.

(For the reason explained under ==.)

?- 6+X=6+3.
X = 3

(Binding *X* to 3 makes the two terms identical. They are both 6+3, not the number 9.)

?- likes(X,prolog)=likes(Y,prolog).
X = Y.

(Binding *X* and *Y* makes the terms identical.)

?- likes(X,prolog)=likes(Y,ada).
false.

(No unification can make the atoms *prolog* and *ada* identical.)

Non-Unification Between Two Terms \=

The goal *Term1\=Term2* succeeds if *Term1=Term2* fails, i.e. the two terms cannot be unified. Otherwise it fails.

?- 6+4\=3+7.
true.

?- likes(X,prolog)\=likes(john,Y).
false.

(Because binding *X* to *john* and *Y* to *prolog* will make the terms identical.)

?- likes(X,prolog)\=likes(X,ada).
true.

4.4   Logical Operators

This section gives a brief description of two operators that take arguments that are call terms, i.e. terms that can be regarded as *goals*.

The *not* Operator

Note: in some versions of Prolog **not/1** is defined as an operator. In others it is simply defined as a predicate with one argument. If your Prolog system is one of the latter, you can make it into an operator by means of a directive such as

?-op(1000,fy,not).

For the purposes of this book we will treat **not/1** as a prefix operator.

The prefix operator **not/1** can be placed before any goal to give its negation. The negated goal succeeds if the original goal fails and fails if the original goal succeeds.

The following examples illustrate the use of **not/1.** It is assumed that the database contains the single clause

```
dog(fido).
```

?- not dog(fido).
false.

?- dog(fred).
false.

?- not dog(fred).
true.

?- X=0,X is 0.
X = 0

?- X=0,not X is 0.
false.

The Disjunction Operator

The disjunction operator **;/2** (written as a semicolon character) is used to represent 'or'. It is an infix operator that takes two arguments, both of which are goals. *Goal1;Goal2* succeeds if either *Goal1* or *Goal2* succeeds.

?- 6<3;7 is 5+2.
true.

?- 6*6=:=36;10=8+3.
true.

4.5   More About Operator Precedence

The **op/3** predicate was introduced in Section 4.1. For the purposes of this book, the operators introduced in this chapter are assumed to be automatically declared by the Prolog system with the following values:

Precedence	Type	Operator(s)
1100	xfy	;
1000	fy	not
700	xfx	is < > =< >= =:= =\= = \= == \==
500	yfx	+ -
400	yfx	* / //
200	xfy	∧
200	fy	+ -

These precedence values vary from one Prolog system to another as does the highest precedence value permitted. The lowest precedence value is always zero. Rather confusingly, the lower the precedence value the higher the precedence.

In Section 4.2 it was stated that "operators with relatively high precedence such as * and / are applied before those with lower precedence such as + and -. Operators with the same precedence (e.g. + and -, * and /) are applied from left to right". From the table we can see that the precedence values of the infix operators * and / are both 400 and the precedence value of + and − (when used as infix operators) is 500. When the Prolog system evaluates the expression **A+B*C-D** the operator of highest precedence (lowest value) is * so the product of **B** and **C** is formed first. Next there is a choice whether to apply the + operator or the − operator. As both of these operators have precedence 500, they are applied from left to right, so the value of **A** is added to the value of **B*C** and then the value of **D** is subtracted.

Other principles relating to precedence are:

• A term enclosed in parentheses has precedence zero.
• The precedence of a term is zero, unless its principal functor is an operator.
• The precedence of a term for which the principal functor is an operator is the precedence of the operator.

This explains what happens when the Prolog system evaluates the expression **(A+B)*C-D**. The bracketed expression **(A+B)** has precedence zero, the highest possible precedence, so it is evaluated first. The resulting value is then multiplied by **C**, as * has the next highest precedence value (400) and the result then has **D** subtracted from it as the remaining operator − has the lowest precedence (500).

The operators + and − both appear twice in the table. The infix versions, as in **A+B** or **A-B** have precedence 400 and the prefix versions as in **−A*B** or **+A*B** have precedence 200. This is helpful as it ensures the expression **−A+B** is interpreted as **(-A)+B** rather than **−(A+B)**, which seems desirable.

?- X is 10, Y is 25, Z is -X+Y.
X = 10,
Y = 25,
Z = 15.

As previously noted, there are three types of infix operator **xfx**, **xfy** and **yfx**. There are also two types of prefix operator **fx** and **fy** and two types of postfix operator **xf** and **yf**.

In all cases the **f** indicates the position of the operator when it is used in an expression (**f** stands for functor). For infix operators it is between the two arguments etc. The letters **x** and **y** indicate the position of the arguments to one or both sides of the operator.

The difference between **x** and **y** is the precedence that the arguments of the operator need to have:

- **x** denotes an argument that has a precedence strictly lower than that of the operator
- **y** denotes an argument that has a precedence less than or equal to that of the operator.

The difference between these is often unimportant but in some cases it matters. If in Section 4.4 the **not** operator had wrongly been declared as of type **fx**, and the database contained the single clause

        dog(fido).

then using **not** would still have been possible

?- dog(fido).
true.

?- not dog(fido).
false.

However a double negation such as

?- not not dog(fido).

would have generated a syntax error.

With **not** properly declared as of type **fy** a sequence of two or more **not** operators is permitted:

?- dog(fido).
true.

?- not dog(fido).
false.

?- not not dog(fido).
true.

?- not not not dog(fido).
false.

?- not not not not dog(fido).
true.

Chapter Summary

This chapter introduces operator notation for predicates and describes the operators provided for evaluating and comparing the values of arithmetic expressions, for testing for equality of either arithmetic expressions or terms and for testing for the negation of a goal or the disjunction of two goals.

Practical Exercise 4

(1) This program is based on Animals Program 3, given in Chapter 2.

```
dog(fido). large(fido).
cat(mary). large(mary).
dog(rover). small(rover).
cat(jane). small(jane).
dog(tom). small(tom).
cat(harry).
dog(fred). large(fred).
cat(henry). large(henry).
cat(bill).
cat(steve). large(steve).
large(jim).
large(mike).
large_dog(X):- dog(X),large(X).
small_animal(A):- dog(A),small(A).
small_animal(B):- cat(B),small(B).
chases(X,Y):-
        large_dog(X),small_animal(Y),
        write(X),write(' chases '),write(Y),nl.
```

Convert the seven predicates used to operator form and test your revised program. The output should be the same as the output from the program above. Include directives to define the operators in your program.

(2) Define and test a predicate which takes two arguments, both numbers, and calculates and outputs the following values: (a) their average, (b) the square root of their product and (c) the larger of (a) and (b).

Chapter 5
Input and Output

Chapter Aims

After reading this chapter you should be able to:

- Use the built-in predicates that read from and write to either the user's terminal (keyboard and screen) or a file, both term by term and character-by-character in your own programs
- Use ASCII values to manipulate strings of characters.

5.1 Introduction

Prolog has facilities to enable input and output either of terms or of characters. Using terms is simpler and will be described first. Initially, it will be assumed that all output is to the user's screen and all input is from the user's keyboard. Input and output using external files, e.g. on a hard disk or CD-ROM, will be described in Section 5.8 onwards. Note that, like many other built-in predicates, those for input and output described in this chapter are all *unresatisfiable*, i.e. they always fail when backtracking.

5.2 Outputting Terms

The main built-in predicate provided for outputting terms is **write/1**, which has already been used many times in this book.

The **write/1** predicate takes a single argument, which must be a valid Prolog term. Evaluating the predicate causes the term to be written to the *current output stream*, which by default is the user's screen. (The meaning of *current output stream* will be explained in Sections 5.8 and 5.9. At present it can simply be taken to mean the user's screen.)

M. Bramer, *Logic Programming with Prolog*, DOI 10.1007/978-1-4471-5487-7_5,
© Springer-Verlag London 2013

The built-in predicate **nl/0** has also been used many times previously in this book. It takes no arguments. Evaluating a **nl** goal causes a new line to be output to the current output stream.

Examples

?- write(26),nl.
26
true.

?- write('a string of characters'),nl.
a string of characters
true.

?- write([a,b,c,d,[x,y,z]]),nl.
[a,b,c,d,[x,y,z]]
true.

?- write(mypred(a,b,c)),nl.
mypred(a,b,c)
true.

?- write('Example of use of nl'),nl,nl,write('end of example'),nl.
Example of use of nl

end of example
true.

Note that atoms that have to be quoted on input (e.g. 'Paul', 'hello world') are not quoted when output using **write**. If it is important to output the quotes, the **writeq/1** predicate can be used. It is identical to **write/1** except that atoms that need quotes for input are output between quotes (other atoms are not).

?- writeq('a string of characters'),nl.
'a string of characters'
true.

?-writeq(dog),nl.
dog
true.

?- writeq('dog'),nl.
dog
true.

5.3 Inputting Terms

The built-in predicate **read/1** is provided to input terms. It takes a single argument, which must be a variable.

Evaluating it causes the next term to be read from the *current input stream*, which by default is the user's keyboard. (The meaning of *current input stream* will be explained in Sections 5.8 and 5.10. At present it can simply be taken to mean the user's keyboard.)

In the input stream, the term must be followed by a dot ('.') and at least one *white space character*, such as space or newline. The dot and white space characters are read in but are not considered part of the term.

> Note that for input from the keyboard a 'prompt' such as |: (a vertical bar followed by a colon) will usually be displayed to indicate that user input is required. The input term has to be followed by a full stop. It will probably also be necessary to press the 'return' key before Prolog will accept the input.

When a **read** goal is evaluated, the input term is *unified* with the argument variable. If the variable is unbound (which is usually the case) it is bound to the input value.

```
?- read(X).
|:jim.
X = jim

?- read(X).
|:26.
X = 26

?- read(X).
|:mypred(a,b,c).
X = mypred(a,b,c)

?- read(Z).
|: [a,b,mypred(p,q,r),[z,y,x]].
Z = [a,b,mypred(p,q,r),[z,y,x]]

?- read(Y).
|: 'a string of characters'.
Y = 'a string of characters'
```

If the argument variable is already bound (which for most users is far more likely to occur by mistake than by design), the goal succeeds if and only if the input term is identical to the previously bound value.

?- X=fred,read(X).
|:jim.
false.

?- X=fred,read(X).
|:fred.
X = fred

5.4   Input and Output Using Characters

Although input and output of terms is straightforward, the use of quotes and full stops can be cumbersome and is not always suitable. For example, it would be tedious to define a predicate (using **read**) which would read a series of characters from the keyboard and count the number of vowels. A much better approach for problems of this kind is to input a character at a time. To do this it is first necessary to know about the *ASCII value* of a character.

All printing characters and many non-printing characters (such as space and tab) have a corresponding ASCII (American Standard Code for Information Interchange) value, which is an integer from 0 to 255.

The table below gives the numerical ASCII values corresponding to the main printable characters and some others.

9	tab	40	(	59	;	94	^
10	end of record	41	)	60	<	95	_
32	space	42	*	61	=	96	`
33	!	43	+	62	>	97–122	a to z
34	"	44	,	63	?		
35	#	45	-	64	@	123	{
36	$	46	.	65-90	A to Z	124		
37	%	47	/	91	[	125	}
38	&	48-57	0 to 9	92	\	126	~
39	'	58	:	93	]		

Characters whose ASCII value is less than or equal to 32 are known as *white space characters*.

5.5   Outputting Characters

Characters are output using the built-in predicate **put/1.** The predicate takes a single argument, which must be a number from 0 to 255 or an expression that evaluates to an integer in that range.

Evaluating a **put** goal causes a single character to be output to the current output stream. This is the character corresponding to the numerical value (ASCII value) of its argument, for example

?- put(97),nl.
a
true.

?- put(122),nl.
z
true.

?- put(64),nl.
@
true.

5.6   Inputting Characters

Two built-in predicates are provided to input a single character: **get0/1** and **get/1**. The **get0** predicate takes a single argument, which must be a variable. Evaluating a **get0** goal causes a character to be read from the current input stream. The variable is then *unified* with the ASCII value of this character.

Note that for input from the keyboard a 'prompt' such as **|:** (a vertical bar followed by a colon) will usually be displayed to indicate that user input is required. It will probably also be necessary to press the 'return' key before Prolog will accept the input. This also applies to the **get** predicate described below.

Assuming the argument variable is unbound (which will usually be the case), it is bound to the ASCII value of the input character.

?- get0(N).
|: a
N = 97

?- get0(N).
|: Z
N = 90

?- get0(M)
|:)
M = 41

If the argument variable is already bound, the goal succeeds if and only if it has a numerical value that is equal to the ASCII value of the input character.

?- M is 41,get0(M).
|:)
M = 41

?- M is 50,get0(M).
|:)
false.

The **get** predicate takes a single argument, which must be a variable. Evaluating a **get** goal causes the next *non-white-space* character (i.e. character with an ASCII value less than or equal to 32) to be read from the current input stream. The variable is then *unified* with the ASCII value of this character in the same way as for **get0**.

?- get(X).
|: Z
X = 90

?- get(M).
|:   Z
M = 90

5.7   Using Characters: Examples

The first example shows how to read in a series of characters from the keyboard finishing with * and to output their corresponding ASCII values one per line (for all characters excluding *).

The predicate **readin** is defined *recursively*. It causes a single character to be input and variable **X** to be bound to its (numerical) ASCII value. The action taken (the **process(X)** goal) depends on whether or not **X** has the value 42 signifying a * character. If it has, the evaluation of the goal stops. If not, the value of **X** is output, followed by a new line, followed by a further call to **readin**. This process goes on indefinitely until a * character is read. (In the example below, the ASCII values of characters P, r, o etc. are correctly shown to be 80, 114, 111 etc.)

```
readin:-get0(X),process(X).
process(42).
process(X):-X=\=42,write(X),nl,readin.
```

?- readin.
|: Prolog Example*
80

114
111
108
111
103
32
69
120
97
109
112
108
101
true.

The next example is an extended version of the one above. This time the ASCII values of the input characters are not output, but the *number* of characters (excluding the *) is output. The **count** predicate is defined with two arguments which can be read as 'the number of characters counted so far' and 'the total number of characters before the *'.

```
go(Total):-count(0,Total).
count(Oldcount,Result):-
    get0(X),process(X,Oldcount,Result).
process(42,Oldcount,Oldcount).
process(X,Oldcount,Result):-
    X=\=42,New is Oldcount+1,count(New,Result).
```

?- go(T).
|: The time has come the walrus said*
T = 33

?- go(T)
|:*
T = 0

The final example is a recursive program, based on the previous two, which shows how to read in a series of characters ending with * and count the number of vowels. Characters are read in one by one until a character with ASCII value 42 (signifying *) is encountered.

Here the two arguments of the **count** predicate can be interpreted as 'the number of vowels so far' and 'the total number of vowels'. The three arguments of the **process** predicate can be read as 'the ASCII value of an input character', 'the number of vowels up to but not including that character' and 'the total number of vowels', respectively.

The first two arguments of the **processChar** predicate can be interpreted in the same way as for **process,** but the third argument is 'the number of vowels up to and including the character (first argument)'.

Predicate **vowel** tests for one of the 10 possible vowels (five upper case and five lower case), using their ASCII values.

```
go(Vowels):-count(0,Vowels).
count(Oldvowels,Totvowels):-
   get0(X),process(X,Oldvowels,Totvowels).
process(42,Oldvowels,Oldvowels).
process(X,Oldvowels,Totalvowels):-
   X=\=42,processChar(X,Oldvowels,New),
   count(New,Totalvowels).
processChar(X,Oldvowels,New):-vowel(X),
   New is Oldvowels+1.
processChar(X,Oldvowels,Oldvowels).
vowel(65)./* A */
vowel(69)./* E */
vowel(73)./* I */
vowel(79)./* O */
vowel(85)./* U */
vowel(97)./* a */
vowel(101)./* e */
vowel(105)./* i */
vowel(111)./* o */
vowel(117)./* u */
```

?- go(Vowels).
|: In the beginning was the word*
Vowels = 8

?- go(Vowels).
|: pqrst*
Vowels = 0

5.8   Input and Output Using Files

Prolog takes all input from the *current input stream* and writes all output to the *current output stream.* By default both of these are the stream named *user,* denoting the user's *terminal,* i.e. keyboard for input and screen for output.

The same facilities available for input and output from and to the user's terminal either term by term or character by character are also available for input and output from and to files (e.g. files on a hard disk or a CD-ROM).

The user may open and close input and output streams associated with any number of named files but there can only be one current input stream and one current output stream at any time. Note that no file can be open for both input and output at the same time (except *user*) and that the *user* input and output streams cannot be closed.

5.9   File Output: Changing the Current Output Stream

The current output stream can be changed using the **tell/1** predicate. This takes a single argument, which is an atom or variable representing a file name, e.g. **tell('outfile.txt').**

Evaluating a **tell** goal causes the named file to become the current output stream. If the file is not already open, a file with the specified name is first created (any existing file with the same name is deleted).

Note that the file corresponding to the previous current output stream remains open when a new current output stream is selected. Only the current output stream can be closed (using the **told** predicate described below).

The default current output stream is *user*, i.e. the user's terminal. This value can be restored either by using the **told** predicate or by **tell(user).**

The built-in predicate **told/0** takes no arguments. Evaluating a **told** goal causes the current output file to be closed and the current output stream to be reset to *user*, i.e. the user's terminal.

The built-in predicate **telling/1** takes one argument, which must be a variable and will normally be unbound. Evaluating a **telling** goal causes the variable to be bound to the name of the current output stream.

Output to a File

Although the above definition of **tell** states that 'any existing file with the same name is deleted', there is another possible requirement, which is important for some applications, namely that the file is not deleted and any output is placed after the end of the existing contents of the file. Both the 'overwrite' and the 'append' options are likely to be available in any practical implementation of Prolog but may involve using a different predicate (e.g. **append/1**) instead of **tell**. See the documentation of your version of Prolog for details.

5.10   File Input: Changing the Current Input Stream

The current input stream can be changed using the **see/1** predicate. This takes a single argument, which is an atom or variable representing a file name, e.g. **see('myfile.txt').**

Evaluating a **see** goal causes the named file to become the current input stream. If the file is not already open it is first opened (for read access only). If it is not possible to open a file with the given name, an error will be generated.

Note that the file corresponding to the previous current input stream remains open when a new current input stream is selected. Only the current input stream can be closed (using the **seen** predicate described below).

The default current input stream is *user*, i.e. the user's terminal. This value can be restored either by using the **seen** predicate or by **see(user).**

The built-in predicate **seen/0** takes no arguments. Evaluating a **seen** goal causes the current input file to be closed and the current input stream to be reset to *user*, i.e. the user's terminal.

The built-in predicate **seeing/1** takes one argument, which must be a variable and will normally be unbound. Evaluating a **seeing** goal causes the variable to be bound to the name of the current input stream.

5.10.1   Reading from Files: End of File

If the end of file is encountered when evaluating the goal **read(X)**, variable **X** will be bound to the atom *end_of_file*.

If the end of file is encountered while evaluating the goal **get(X)** or **get0(X)**, variable **X** will be bound to a 'special' numerical value. As ASCII values must be in the range 0 to 255 inclusive, this will typically be −1, but may vary from one implementation of Prolog to another.

5.10.2   Reading from Files: End of Record

The end of a line of input at the user's terminal and the end of a record in a file will typically both be indicated by the ASCII value 10 and that is the assumption we will make in this book. In some Prolog systems different values are used. (For example the end of a line of input at the user's terminal is sometimes represented by 13 and the end of a record in a file is sometimes represented by two ASCII values: 13 followed by 10.)

The following program shows how to read in a series of characters from the keyboard and print them out, one per line.

```
readline:-get0(X),process(X).
process(10).
process(X):-X=\=10,put(X),nl,readline.
```

Note the use of **put** rather than **write** and that the test for ASCII value 10 avoids the need for a character such as * to indicate 'end of input'.

?- readline.
|: Prolog test
P
r
o
l
o
g

t
e
s
t

5.11 Using Files: Examples

Example 1

Adapt the final program given in Section 5.7 to read the characters in a text file *myfile.txt* until a * character is reached and output the number of vowels to the user's terminal (i.e. the screen).

Only the first line of the previous program needs to be changed, to:

```
go(Vowels):-see('myfile.txt'),count(0,Vowels),seen.
```

Example 2

Define a predicate **readterms** to read the first four terms from a specified file and output them to another specified file, one per line.

A suitable definition is given below.

```
readterms(Infile,Outfile):-
    see(Infile),tell(Outfile),
    read(T1),write(T1),nl,read(T2),write(T2),nl,
    read(T3),write(T3),nl,read(T4),write(T4),nl,
    seen,told.
```

Assuming the contents of file *textfile.txt* are the three lines:

'first term'. 'second term'.
'third term'.
'fourth term'. 'fifth term'.

---

using **readterms** gives the following brief output:

?- readterms('textfile.txt','outfile.txt').
true.

and creates a file with four lines of text

---

first term
second term
third term
fourth term

Although the definition of **readterms** above is correct as far as it goes, the final two terms (**seen** and **told**) will cause the current input and output streams to be set to *user*. This could cause problems if **readterms** were used as a subgoal in a larger program where the current input and output streams were not necessarily both *user* when it was called.

It is good programming practice to restore the original input and output streams as the final steps when a goal such as **readterms** is evaluated. This can be achieved for input by placing the goals **seeing(S)** and **see(S)** before and after the other terms in the body of a rule. The former binds **S** to the name of the current input stream; the latter resets the current input stream to **S.**

A similar effect can achieved for output by placing the goals **telling(T)** and **tell(T)** before and after the other terms in the body of a rule. The former binds **T** to the name of the current output stream; the latter resets the current output stream to **T.**

Using these conventions, the revised definition of **readterms** is as follows:

```
readterms(Infile,Outfile):-
    seeing(S),see(Infile),telling(T),tell(Outfile),
    read(T1),write(T1),nl,read(T2),write(T2),nl,
    read(T3),write(T3),nl,read(T4),write(T4),nl,
    seen,see(S),told,tell(T).
```

Example 3

Define a predicate **copychars** to copy characters input (as a single line) at the user's terminal to a specified file, until the character **!** is entered (this character should not be copied).

In the program below, **copychars** mainly saves and restores the values of the current input and output streams. The rest of the task is left to **copy_characters,** which is defined recursively in a similar way to **readin** in the first example in Section 5.7.

```
copychars(Outfile):- telling(T),tell(Outfile),
    copy_characters,told,tell(T).
copy_characters:-get0(N),process(N).
/* 33 is ASCII value of character ! */
process(33).
process(N):-N=\=33,put(N),copy_characters.
```

Using **copychars** as follows

?- copychars('myfile.txt').
|: abxyz!
true.

will place the characters *abxyz* in file *myfile.txt.*

Chapter Summary

Describes the principal built-in predicates available for both term by term and character by character input and output and for reading and writing files. Also introduces the notion of the ASCII value of a character.

Practical Exercise 5

(1) Define a predicate **makelower/0** which reads in a line of characters from the keyboard and outputs it again as a single line with any upper case letters converted to lower case. (The ASCII values of the characters *a*, *z*, *A* and *Z* are 97, 122, 65 and 90, respectively.)

Thus the following would be a typical use of **makelower**:

?- makelower.
|: This is an Example 123 inCLUDing numbers and symbols +−*/@[] XYz
this is an example 123 including numbers and symbols +−*/@[] xyz

(2) Define a predicate **copyterms** which reads all the terms in a text file and outputs
them as terms to another text file one by one on separate lines.

The output file should be in a format suitable for use as the input file in a
subsequent call of **copyterms**. Thus for example if the input file contained

```
'first term'. 'second term'.
'third term'.

fourth. 'fifth term'.
sixth.
```

The output file would contain

```
'first term'.
'second term'.
'third term'.
fourth.
'fifth term'.
sixth.
```

(3) Create a text file *testa.txt* containing two lines, each of five characters followed
by a new line, e.g.

```
abcde
fghij
```

Define a predicate **readfile** that will read *thirteen* characters from this file one by
one and output the ASCII value of each character. Use this to establish whether the
representations of 'end of file' and 'end of record' for your version of Prolog are as
suggested in Sections 5.10.1 and 5.10.2, respectively.

(4) Using a text editor, create two text files *in1.txt* and *in2.txt,* each comprising a
number of terms terminated by *end*.

Define and test a predicate **combine** that takes the names of two input files as its first two arguments and the name of an output file as its third argument. The output file should contain the terms in the first input file followed by the terms in the second, one per line and terminated by *end*.

(5) Define and test a predicate **compare** that reads in two text files term by term and for each pair of corresponding terms outputs a message either saying that they are the same or that they are different. Assume that both files contain the same number of terms and that the final term in each is *end*.

Chapter 6
Loops

Chapter Aims

After reading this chapter you should be able to:

- Define a predicate which causes a sequence of goals to be evaluated repeatedly, either a fixed number of times or until a specified condition is satisfied
- Define a predicate which searches a database to find all the clauses with a specified property.

6.1 Introduction

Most conventional programming languages have a *looping* facility that enables a set of instructions to be executed repeatedly either a fixed number of times or until a given condition is met. Although, as was pointed out in the introduction to this book, Prolog has no looping facilities, similar effects can be obtained that enable a sequence of goals to be evaluated repeatedly. This can be done in a variety of ways, using backtracking, recursion, built-in predicates, or a combination of these.

6.2 Looping a Fixed Number of Times

Many programming languages provide 'for loops' which enable a set of instructions to be executed a fixed number of times. No such facility is available in Prolog (directly), but a similar effect can be obtained using recursion, as shown in the example programs below.

Example 1

The following program outputs integers from a specified value down to 1.

M. Bramer, *Logic Programming with Prolog*, DOI 10.1007/978-1-4471-5487-7_6,
© Springer-Verlag London 2013

```
loop(0).

loop(N):-N>0,write('The value is: '),write(N),nl,
   M is N-1,loop(M).
```

The **loop** predicate is defined in terms of itself. The second clause can be thought of as: 'to loop from **N**, first write the value of **N**, then subtract one to give **M**, then loop from **M**'. This process clearly needs to be terminated and this is achieved by the first clause: 'when the argument is zero, do nothing (and hence stop)'. The first clause can be regarded as a *terminating condition* for the recursion.

?- loop(6).
The value is: 6
The value is: 5
The value is: 4
The value is: 3
The value is: 2
The value is: 1
true.

Note the use of the two goals **M is N-1,loop(M)** in the second clause for the **loop** predicate. The obvious alternative of **loop(N-1)** will not work. Prolog only evaluates expressions such as **N-1** when evaluating goals with functor **is** or one of the relational operators, as described in Chapter 4. If **N-1** is used as an argument of a predicate it is taken to mean the term with infix operator **-** (i.e. a minus sign) and arguments **N** and **1.** This is most unlikely to be what is intended!

Example 2

The next program outputs integers from *First* to *Last* inclusive.

```
/* output integers from First to Last inclusive */
output_values(Last,Last):- write(Last),nl,
   write('end of example'),nl.

output_values(First,Last):-First=\=Last,write
   (First),nl,N is First+1,output_values(N,Last).
```

Here **output_values** has two arguments, which can be read as 'output the integers from *First* to *Last* inclusive'. The loop terminates when both arguments are the same.

?- output_values(5,12).
5
6

7
8
9
10
11
12
end of example
true.

Example 3

Define a predicate to find the sum of the integers from 1 to N (say for N = 100).

It is natural to think of this procedurally, i.e. start with 1, then add 2, then add 3, then add 4, ... , then add 100. However the process is much easier to program if re-expressed declaratively in terms of itself.

The sum of the first 100 integers is the sum of the first 99 integers, plus 100.
The sum of the first 99 integers is the sum of the first 98 integers, plus 99.
The sum of the first 98 integers is the sum of the first 97 integers, plus 98.

....

The sum of the first 3 integers is the sum of the first 2 integers, plus 3.
The sum of the first 2 integers is the sum of the first 1 integers, plus 2.
The sum of the first 1 integers is one.

There are two distinct cases to consider: the *general case:* 'the sum of the first N integers is the sum of the first N-1 integers, plus N' and the *terminating case:* 'the sum of the first 1 integers is 1'. This leads directly to the recursive definition:

```
/* sum the integers from 1 to N (the first argument)
inclusive */
sumto(1,1).

sumto(N,S):-N>1,N1 is N-1,sumto(N1,S1),S is S1+N.
```

?- sumto(100,N).
N = 5050

?- sumto(1,1).
true.

Note that using the additional variable **N1** for holding the value of **N-1** is essential. Writing **sumto(N-1,S1)** etc. instead would not work correctly. **N-1** is a term, not a numerical value.

Example 4

Define a predicate to output the squares of the first N integers, one per line.
   This can most easily be programmed if first recast in a recursive form, as follows.

To output the squares of the first N integers, output the squares of the first N-1 and
   then output N^2
To output the squares of the first N-1 integers, output the squares of the first N-2 and
   then output $(N-1)^2$
To output the squares of the first N-2 integers, output the squares of the first N-3 and
   then output $(N-2)^2$

....

To output the squares of the first 3 integers, output the squares of the first 2 and then
   output 3^2
To output the squares of the first 2 integers, output the squares of the first 1 and then
   output 2^2
To output the squares of the first 1 integers, output the number 1

   Here the general case is 'to output the squares of the first N integers, output the
squares of the first $N-1$ and then output N^2' and the terminating case is 'to output
the squares of the first 1 integers, output the number 1'. This leads to the following
two-clause program.

```
/* output the first N squares, one per line */
writesquares(1):-write(1),nl.

writesquares(N):-N>1,N1 is N-1,writesquares(N1),
    Nsq is N*N,write(Nsq),nl.
```

?- writesquares(6).
1
4
9
16
25
36
true

Example 5

The following program reads the first 6 terms from a specified file and writes them
to the current output stream. It uses a 'counting down' method, in a similar way to
Example 1.

```
read_six(Infile):-seeing(S),see(Infile),

process_terms(6),seen,see(S).
process_terms(0).
process_terms(N):-N>0,read(X),write(X),nl,N1 is N-1,
process_terms(N1).
```

6.3 Looping Until a Condition Is Satisfied

Many languages have an 'until loop' which enables a set of instructions to be executed repeatedly until a given condition is met. Again, no such facility is available directly in Prolog, but a similar effect can be obtained in several ways.

6.3.1 Recursion

The first example below shows the use of recursion to read terms entered by the user from the keyboard and output them to the screen, until *end* is encountered.

```
go:-loop(start). /* start is a dummy value used to
get the looping process started.*/

loop(end).
loop(X):-X\=end,write('Type end to end: '),read(Word),
    write('Input was '),write(Word),nl,loop(Word).
```

?- go.
Type end to end: university.
Input was university
Type end to end: of.
Input was of
Type end to end: portsmouth.
Input was portsmouth
Type end to end: end.
Input was end
true.

Using the disjunction operator **;/2** which was defined in Section 4.4 the above program can be rewritten as a single clause.

```
loop:-write('Type end to end: '),read(Word),
    write('Input was '),write(Word),nl,
    (Word=end;loop).
```

The 'disjunctive goal' (**Word=end;loop**) succeeds if variable *Word* is bound to the atom *end*. If not, the system attempts to satisfy the goal **loop** recursively.

?- loop.
Type end to end: university.
Input was university
Type end to end: of.
Input was of
Type end to end: portsmouth.
Input was portsmouth
Type end to end: end.
Input was end
true.

This recursive program repeatedly prompts the user to enter a term until either *yes* or *no* is entered.

```
get_answer(Ans):-write('Enter answer to question'),
    nl,get_answer2(Ans).
```

```
get_answer2(Ans):-
    write('answer yes or no: '),
    read(A),
    ((valid(A),Ans=A,write('Answer is '),
    write(A),nl);get_answer2(Ans)).
    valid(yes). valid(no).
```

?- get_answer(Myanswer).
Enter answer to question
answer yes or no: maybe.
answer yes or no: possibly.
answer yes or no: yes.
Answer is yes
Myanswer = yes

6.3.2 Using the 'repeat' Predicate

Although it can often be used to great effect, recursion is not always the easiest way to provide the types of looping required in Prolog programs. Another method that is often used is based on the built-in predicate **repeat.**

The name of this predicate is really a misnomer. The goal **repeat** does not repeat anything; it merely succeeds whenever it is called. The great value of **repeat** is that it also succeeds (as many times as necessary) on backtracking. The effect of this, as for any other goal succeeding, is to change the order of evaluating goals from 'right to left' (i.e. backtracking) back to 'left-to-right'. This can be used to create a looping effect, as shown in the examples below.

This program repeatedly prompts the user to enter a term until either *yes* or *no* is entered. It is an alternative to the recursive program shown at the end of the previous section. In this case it is debatable whether using **repeat** is an improvement on using recursion, but the example is included for purposes of illustration.

```
get_answer(Ans):-
    write('Enter answer to question'),nl,
    repeat,write('answer yes or no: '),read(Ans),
    valid(Ans),write('Answer is '),write(Ans),nl.

valid(yes). valid(no).
```

The first five goals in the body of **get_answer** will always succeed. Evaluating the fifth goal: **read(Ans)** will prompt the user to enter a term. If the term input is anything but *yes* or *no*, say *unsure*, the following goal **valid(Ans)** will fail. Prolog will then backtrack over **read(Ans)** and **write('answer yes or no')**, both of which are *unresatisfiable*, i.e. will always fail on backtracking.

Backtracking will then reach the predicate **repeat** and succeed, causing evaluation to proceed forward (left-to-right) again, with **write('answer yes or no')** and **read(Ans)** both succeeding, followed by a further evaluation of **valid(Ans).**

Depending on the value of **Ans,** i.e. the user's input, the **valid(Ans)** goal will either fail, in which case Prolog will backtrack as far as **repeat,** as before, or it will succeed in which case the final three goals **write('Answer is')**, **write(Ans)** and **nl** will all succeed. The overall effect is that the two goals **write('answer yes or no')** and **read(Ans)** are called repeatedly until the terminating condition **valid(Ans)** is satisfied, effectively creating a loop between **repeat** and **valid(Ans).**

?- get_answer(X).
Enter answer to question
answer yes or no: unsure.
answer yes or no: possibly.
answer yes or no: no.
answer is no
X = no

Goals to the left of **repeat** in the body of a clause will never be reached on backtracking.

The next program reads a sequence of terms from a specified file and outputs them to the current output stream until the term *end* is encountered.

```
readterms(Infile):-
    seeing(S),see(Infile),
    repeat,read(X),write(X),nl,X=end,
    seen,see(S).
```

In a similar way to the previous program, this effectively defines a loop between the goals **repeat** and **X=end.**

If file *myfile.txt* contains the lines

```
'first term'. 'second term'.
'third term'. 'fourth term'.
'fifth term'. 'sixth term'.
'seventh term'.
'eighth term'.
end.
```

calling **readterms** will produce the following output

?- readterms('myfile.txt').
first term
second term
third term
fourth term
fifth term
sixth term
seventh term
eighth term
end
true.

This program shows how to implement a menu structure which loops back repeatedly to request more input. Entering **go** at the prompt causes Prolog to output a menu from which the user can choose activities one at a time until option *d* is chosen. Note that all inputs are terms and so must be followed by a full stop character.

```
go:- write('This shows how a repeated menu works'),
    menu.

menu:-nl,write('MENU'),nl,
    write('a. Activity A'),nl,write('b. Activity B'),nl,
    write('c. Activity C'),nl,write('d. End'),nl,

read(Choice),nl,choice(Choice).

choice(a):-write('Activity A chosen'),menu.
choice(b):-write('Activity B chosen'),menu.
choice(c):-write('Activity C chosen'),menu.
choice(d):-write('Goodbye!'),nl.
choice(_):-write('Please try again!'),menu.
```

?- go.
This shows how a repeated menu works
MENU
a. Activity A
b. Activity B
c. Activity C
d. End
: b.

Activity B chosen
MENU
a. Activity A
b. Activity B
c. Activity C
d. End
: xxx.

Please try again!
MENU
a. Activity A
b. Activity B
c. Activity C
d. End
: d.

Goodbye!
true.

6.4   Backtracking with Failure

As the name implies, the predicate **fail** always fails, whether on 'standard' evaluation left-to-right or on backtracking. Advantage can be taken of this, combined with Prolog's automatic backtracking, to search through the database to find all the clauses with a specified property.

6.4.1   Searching the Prolog Database

Supposing the database contains clauses such as

```
dog(fido).
dog(fred).
dog(jonathan).
```

Each **dog** clause can be processed in turn using the **alldogs** predicate defined below.

```
alldogs:-dog(X),write(X),write(' is a dog'),nl,fail.
alldogs.
```

Calling **alldogs** will cause **dog(X)** to be matched with the **dog** clauses in the database. Initially **X** will be bound to *fido* and 'fido is a dog' will be output. The final goal in the first clause of the **alldogs** predicate will then cause evaluation to fail. Prolog will then backtrack over **nl** and the two **write** goals (all of which are unresatisfiable) until it reaches **dog(X)**. This goal will succeed for a second time causing **X** to be bound to *fred*.

This process will continue until *fido, fred* and *jonathan* have all been output, when evaluation will again fail. This time the call to **dog(X)** will also fail as there are no further **dog** clauses in the database. This will cause the first clause for **alldogs** to fail and Prolog to examine the second clause of **alldogs**. This will succeed and evaluation will stop.

The effect is to loop through the database finding all possible values of **X** that satisfy the goal **dog(X)**.

?- alldogs.
fido is a dog
fred is a dog
jonathan is a dog
true.

Note the importance of the second clause of the **alldogs** predicate. It is there to ensure that, after the database has been searched, the goal succeeds. With only the first line, any call to **alldogs** will eventually fail.

```
alldogs:-dog(X),write(X),write(' is a dog'),nl,fail.
```

?- alldogs.
fido is a dog
fred is a dog
jonathan is a dog
false.

The next program is designed to search a database containing clauses representing the name, age, place of residence and occupation of a number of people.

If the database contains these five clauses

```
person(john,smith,45,london,doctor).
person(martin,williams,33,birmingham,teacher).
person(henry,smith,26,manchester,plumber).
person(jane,wilson,62,london,teacher).
person(mary,smith,29,glasgow,surveyor).
```

The names of all the teachers can be found using the **allteachers** predicate.

```
allteachers:-person(Forename,Surname,_,_,teacher),
    write(Forename),write(' '),write(Surname),nl,
    fail.

allteachers.
```

The effect of using backtracking with failure in this case is to find all the teachers in the database.

?- allteachers.
martin williams
jane wilson
true.

If the second clause of **allteachers** were omitted, both teachers would still be found but the evaluation of **allteachers** would end with failure. This is of little or no importance when a goal is entered at the system prompt, but if **allteachers** were used as a goal in the body of a rule it would obviously be desirable to ensure that it always succeeded.

It should be noted that it is not always necessary to use 'backtracking with failure' to search the database. For example, the predicate **somepeople/0** defined below will find all the people in the database given previously, down to *williams,* using only standard backtracking.

```
somepeople:-person(Forename,Surname,_,_,_),
    write(Forename),write(' '),write(Surname),nl,
    Surname=williams.

somepeople.
```

The goal **Surname=williams** succeeds if the variable *Surname* is bound to *williams.* If not, it fails. The effect is to search the database down to and including the **person** clause with second argument *williams.*

?- somepeople.
john smith
martin williams
true.

6.4.2   *Finding Multiple Solutions*

Backtracking with failure can also be used to find all the ways of satisfying a goal. Suppose that a predicate **findroute(Town1,Town2,Route)** finds a route *Route* between two towns *Town1* and *Town2*. The details of this predicate are irrelevant here. It may be assumed that *Town1* and *Town2* are atoms and that *Route* is a list.

Backtracking with failure can then be used to find all possible routes between *Town1* and *Town2* and write out each one on a separate line, as follows:

```
find_all_routes(Town1,Town2):-
    findroute(Town1,Town2,Route),
    write('Possible route: '),write(Route),nl,fail.

find_all_routes(_,_).
```

Chapter Summary

This chapter describes how a set of goals can be evaluated repeatedly in Prolog, either a fixed number of times or until a specified condition is met, and how multiple solutions can be arrived at using the technique of 'backtracking with failure'.

Practical Exercise 6

(1) Define a predicate to output the values of the squares of the integers from N1 to N2 inclusive and test it with N1 = 6 and N2 = 12.

(2) Define and test a predicate to read in a series of characters input by the user and output all of those before the first new line or ? character.

(3) Using the **person** clauses given in Section 6.4.1, find the professions of all those over 40.

Chapter 7
Preventing Backtracking

Chapter Aims

After reading this chapter you should be able to:

- Use the cut predicate to prevent unwanted backtracking
- Use 'cut with failure' to specify exceptions to general rules.

7.1 Introduction

Backtracking (as described in Chapter 3) is a fundamental part of the process by which the Prolog system satisfies goals. However, it can sometimes be too powerful and lead to inappropriate results. This chapter is about preventing the Prolog system from backtracking using a built-in predicate called *cut*, which is written as an exclamation mark ! character.

Before going on, it is worth issuing a warning. Many Prolog users see preventing backtracking using 'cut' as being 'against the spirit of the language' and some would even like to see it banned altogether! It is included in the language (and in this book) because it can sometimes be very useful. When used badly, it can also be a cause of programming errors that are very hard to find. The best advice is probably to use it only sparingly and with care.

7.2 The Cut Predicate

We start by giving two examples of predicate definitions that appear correct but give erroneous results when used with backtracking.

M. Bramer, *Logic Programming with Prolog*, DOI 10.1007/978-1-4471-5487-7_7,
© Springer-Verlag London 2013

Example 1

The **larger** predicate takes the value of the larger of its first two arguments (which are assumed to be numbers) and returns it as the value of the third.

```
larger(A,B,A):-A>B.
larger(A,B,B).
```

With the usual 'top to bottom' searching of clauses, the second clause can reasonably be assumed to apply only when *A* is less than or equal to *B*. Testing the definition with 8 and 6 as the first two arguments gives the correct answer.

?- larger(8,6,X).
X = 8

However, if the user forces the system to backtrack at this stage, it will go on to examine the second clause for **larger** and generate an incorrect second answer.

?- larger(8,6,X).
X = 8;
X = 6
?-

Example 2

The definition of predicate **sumto/2** given below is a slightly modified version of the one given in Chapter 6. It still appears to be correct, but has a serious flaw.

The goal **sumto(N,S)** causes the sum of the integers from 1 to *N* to be calculated and returns the answer as the value of *S*.

```
sumto(1,1).
sumto(N,S):-N1 is N-1,sumto(N1,S1),
    S is S1+N.
```

?- sumto(3,S).
S = 6

However, forcing backtracking will now cause the system to crash with a cryptic error message, such as 'stack overflow'. Whilst evaluating the goal **sumto(3,S)** the Prolog system will try to find a solution for the goal **sumto(1,S)**. The first time it does this the first clause is used and the second argument is correctly bound to 1. On backtracking the first clause is rejected and the system attempts to satisfy the goal using the second clause. This causes it to subtract one from one and then evaluate the goal **sumto(0,S)**. Doing this will in turn require it to evaluate **sumto(−1,S1)**, then **sumto(−2,S1)** and so on, until eventually the system runs out of memory.

Examples 1 and 2 could both be remedied by using additional goals in the definition of the predicates, e.g. by changing the second clause of the definition of **larger** to

```
larger(A,B,B):-A=<B.
```

and the second clause in the definition of **sumto** to

```
sumto(N,S):-N>1,N1 is N-1,sumto(N1,S1),S is S1+N.
```

However, in other cases identifying such additional terms can be considerably more difficult.

A more general way to avoid unwanted backtracking is to use a *cut*. The goal ! (pronounced 'cut') in the body of a rule always succeeds when first evaluated. On backtracking it always fails and prevents any further evaluation of the current goal, which therefore fails.

Example 1 (revised)

```
larger(A,B,A):-A>B,!.
larger(A,B,B).
```

?- larger(8,6,X).
X = 8
?-

Example 2 (revised)

```
sumto(1,1):-!.
sumto(N,S):-N1 is N-1,sumto(N1,S1),
    S is S1+N.
```

?- sumto(6,S).
S = 21
?-

Note that backtracking over a cut not only causes the evaluation of the current clause of **larger** or **sumto** to be abandoned but also prevents the evaluation of any other clauses for that predicate.

Example 3

The following incorrect program defines a predicate **classify/2** that classifies a number (its first argument) as either positive, negative or zero. The first clause deals explicitly with the case where the first argument is zero. The second deals with a negative value, leaving the third to deal with positive values.

```
/* classify a number as positive, negative or zero */
classify(0,zero).
classify(N,negative):-N<0.
classify(N,positive).
```

However, as before, the absence of a specific test for a positive argument causes problems when the user forces the system to backtrack.

?- classify(0,N).
N = zero;
N = positive

?- classify(−4,X).
X = negative;
X = positive
?-

This can be rectified either by changing the third clause to

```
classify(N,positive):-N>0.
```

or by using cuts.

Example 3 (revised)

```
classify(0,zero):-!.
classify(N,negative):-N<0,!.
classify(N,positive).
```

?- classify(0,N).
N = zero

?- classify(−4,N).
N = negative
?-

So far all the incorrect programs could have been rectified by adding an additional goal to one of the clauses rather than using cuts, and that would probably have been the better approach. The following example shows a more difficult case.

Example 4

A very common requirement is to prompt the user for an answer to a question until a valid answer (e.g. yes or no) is entered. The following program does this using a **repeat** loop, but unhelpfully will continue to prompt for valid answers on backtracking.

```
get_answer(Ans):-
   write('Enter answer to question'),nl,
   repeat,write('answer yes or no: '),read(Ans),
   valid(Ans),write('Answer is '),write(Ans),nl.
valid(yes).
valid(no).
```

?- **get_answer(X).**
Enter answer to question
answer yes or no: maybe.
answer yes or no: yes.
Answer is yes
X = yes;
answer yes or no: no.
Answer is no
X = no;
answer yes or no: unsure.
answer yes or no: yes.
Answer is yes
X = yes

(and so on indefinitely).

Example 4 (revised)

Adding a final cut to the definition of **get_answer** will prevent the unwanted backtracking.

```
get_answer(Ans):-
   write('Enter answer to question'),nl.
   repeat,write('answer yes or no: '),read(Ans),
   valid(Ans),write('Answer is '),write(Ans),nl,!.
valid(yes).
valid(no).
```

?- get_answer(X).
Enter answer to question
answer yes or no: maybe.
answer yes or no: unsure.
answer yes or no: yes.
Answer is yes
X = yes
?-

The above example, like all the other examples in this chapter so far, illustrates the solution to a problem that could have been avoided if the user had not chosen to force the system to backtrack. In practice, it is most unlikely that anyone would want to do so. The prevention of unwanted backtracking is of much more practical importance when one predicate 'calls' another (i.e. makes use of another as a goal in the body of one of its clauses). This can lead to apparently inexplicable results.

Example 5

The **go** predicate in the following program uses a **repeat** loop to prompt the user for input until a positive number is entered. However, the lack of cuts in the definition of the **classify** predicate leads to incorrect answers.

```
classify(0,zero).
classify(N,negative):-N<0.
classify(N,positive).
go:-write(start),nl,
   repeat,write('enter a positive value'),read(N),
   classify(N,Type),Type=positive,
   write('positive value is '),write(N),nl.
```

?- go.
start
enter a positive value: 28.
positive value is 28
true.

?- go.
start
enter a positive value: -6.
positive value is −6
true.

?- go.
start
enter a positive value: 0.

positive value is 0
true.

(In each case the system gives the user the option to backtrack to find more possible solutions. It is assumed that the user presses the 'return' key to suppress backtracking.)

Changing the definition of **classify** to the one given in Example 3 (revised) above and placing a cut at the end of the final clause gives the expected behaviour for **go**.

Example 5 (revised)

```
classify(0,zero):-!.
classify(N,negative):-N<0,!.
classify(N,positive).
go:-write(start),nl,
   repeat,
   write('enter a positive value: '),read(N),
   classify(N,Type),
   Type=positive,
   write('positive value is '),write(N),nl,!.
```

?- go.
start
enter a positive value: -6.
enter a positive value: -7.
enter a positive value: 0.
enter a positive value: 45.
positive value is 45
true.

7.3   Cut with Failure

Another use of 'cut' that can sometimes be helpful is to specify exceptions to general rules.

Suppose that we have a database of the names of birds, such as

```
bird(sparrow).
bird(eagle).
bird(duck).
bird(crow).
```

```
bird(ostrich).
bird(puffin).
bird(swan).
bird(albatross).
bird(starling).
bird(owl).
bird(kingfisher).
bird(thrush).
```

A natural rule to add to this would be

```
can_fly(X):-bird(X).
```

corresponding to 'all birds can fly'.

Unfortunately this rule is over general. There are a few exceptions, notably that ostriches cannot fly. How can we ensure that the goal **can_fly(ostrich)** will always fail? The obvious approach is to change the definition of the **can_fly** predicate to

```
can_fly(ostrich):-fail.
can_fly(X):-bird(X).
```

However this does not give the desired result:

?- can_fly(duck).
true.

?- can_fly(ostrich).
true.

The **can_fly(ostrich)** goal is matched with the head of the first **can_fly** clause. Attempting to satisfy the goal in the body of that clause (i.e. **fail**) obviously fails, so the system next looks at the second **can_fly** clause. The goal matches with the head, and the goal in the body of the clause, i.e. **bird(X)** is also satisfied, so the **can_fly(ostrich)** goal succeeds. This is obviously not what was intended.

The desired effect can be achieved by replacing the **can_fly** clauses by

```
can_fly(ostrich):-!,fail.
can_fly(X):-bird(X).
```

?- can_fly(duck).
true.

?- can_fly(ostrich).
false.

As before, the **can_fly(ostrich)** goal is matched with the head of the first **can_fly** clause. Attempting to satisfy the goal in the body of that clause (i.e. **fail**) fails, but the cut prevents the system from backtracking and so the **can_fly(ostrich)** goal fails.

The combination of goals **!,fail** is known as *cut with failure*.

Chapter Summary

This chapter describes how the 'cut' predicate can be used to prevent undesirable backtracking and how 'cut' can be used in conjunction with the 'fail' predicate to specify exceptions to general rules.

Practical Exercise 7

(1) The predicate defined below is intended to correspond to the mathematical function *factorial*. The factorial of a positive integer N is defined as the product of all the integers from 1 to N inclusive, e.g. the factorial of 6 is $1 \times 2 \times 3 \times 4 \times 5 \times 6 = 720$.

```
factorial(1,1).
factorial(N,Nfact):-N1 is N-1,
    factorial(N1,Nfact1),Nfact is N*Nfact1.
```

The definition of the **factorial** predicate is incorrect as given, and using it can cause the system to crash.

Demonstrate that this definition is incorrect by entering a goal such as **factorial(6,N)**. Use backtracking to try to find more than one solution.

Correct the program and use it to find the factorials of 6 and 7.

(2) The following is part of a program that defines a predicate **go** which prompts the user to input a series of numbers ending with 100 and outputs a message saying whether each is odd or even.

```
go:-repeat,read_and_check(N,Type),
write(N),write(' is '),write(Type),nl,N=:=100.
```

Complete the program by defining the predicate **read_and_check** to obtain output such as that given below. Your program should use at least one cut.

?- go.
Enter next number: 23.
23 is odd

Enter next number: -4.
-4 is even
Enter next number: 13.
13 is odd
Enter next number: 24.
24 is even
Enter next number: 100.
100 is even
true.

Chapter 8
Changing the Prolog Database

Chapter Aims

After reading this chapter you should be able to:

- Define a predicate which causes one or more clauses to be added to or deleted from the Prolog database
- Define predicates to create and manipulate a database of related facts within the Prolog database.

8.1 Changing the Database: Adding and Deleting Clauses

The normal way of placing clauses in the Prolog database is to **consult** a file. This causes all the clauses in the file to be loaded into the database. Any existing clauses for the same predicates are first deleted.

Clauses placed into the database this way normally stay there until replaced by a subsequent **consult**, or until the user exits from the Prolog system when all clauses are automatically deleted. For most purposes this is entirely sufficient. However Prolog also has built-in predicates for adding clauses to and deleting clauses from the database which can be useful for more advanced programming in the language. Like many other advanced features, they need to be used with care. These built-in predicates can be used either in the body of a rule or as directives entered at the system prompt.

As the user's program and the Prolog database are equivalent, using them in the body of a rule can give the effect of modifying the user's program while it is executing.

M. Bramer, *Logic Programming with Prolog*, DOI 10.1007/978-1-4471-5487-7_8,
© Springer-Verlag London 2013

Static and dynamic predicates

If one or more clauses for a predicate, say **mypred/3**, are loaded into the database from a program file using the **consult/1** predicate, the predicate is regarded as *static*.

In this chapter facilities are described to add clauses to the database without using **consult/1** and also to remove predicates from the database. However if these are to be applied to any predicates loaded using **consult** it is first necessary to tell the system to treat the predicates as *dynamic*. This can be done using directives such as

?-dynamic(mypred/3).

The directive should be added (including the ?- prompt) to the program file at or near the start and certainly before the first clause for the **mypred** predicate.

If the **dynamic** directive is left out, attempts to modify the database using the methods described below are likely to produce error messages such as 'Predicate Protected' or 'No permission to modify static procedure'.

(Note that if **consult** is used with one or more 'dynamic' directives in this way, any existing clauses for the predicates specified as dynamic are not automatically deleted when the new clauses are loaded. In this case the new clauses for the 'dynamic' predicates are placed after the existing ones in the database.)

8.2   Adding Clauses

Two main predicates are available for adding clauses to the database. Both take a single argument, which must be a *clause,* i.e. a fact or a rule.

assertz(Clause)

The predicate **assertz/1** causes *Clause* to be added to the database at the end of the sequence of clauses that define the corresponding predicate.

The clause used for the first argument should be written without a terminating full stop. Rules must be enclosed in an additional pair of parentheses, e.g.

?-assertz(dog(fido)).

?-assertz((go:-write('hello world'),nl)).

The clause may include one or more variables, e.g.

?-assertz(dog(X)).

?-assertz((go(X):-write('hello'),write(X),nl)).

asserta(Clause)

The predicate **asserta/1** causes *Clause* to be added to the database at the start of the sequence of clauses that define the corresponding predicate.

The clause used for the first argument should be written without a terminating full stop. Rules must be enclosed in an additional pair of parentheses, e.g.

?-asserta(dog(fido)).

?-asserta((go:-write('hello world'),nl)).

8.3   Deleting Clauses

Two main predicates are available for deleting clauses from the database.

retract(Clause)

The predicate **retract/1** takes a single argument, which must be a *clause,* i.e. a fact or a rule. It causes the first clause in the database that matches (i.e. unifies with) *Clause* to be deleted.

If the user's program file contains

```
?-dynamic(dog/1).
dog(jim).
dog(fido).
dog(henry).
dog(X).
```

consulting the file places the four **dog** clauses in the database and makes predicate **dog** 'dynamic'. Now the query

?-retract(dog(fido)).

will delete the second clause and the further query

?-retract(dog(X)).

will delete the **dog(jim)** clause, which is the *first* one of the remaining clauses to unify with the query. The system will pause to allow the user to force it to backtrack. We will assume that the user presses the 'return' key to suppress backtracking at this point.

This will leave the **dog(henry)** and **dog(X)** clauses in the database. Although unusual, the latter is a valid Prolog fact which signifies 'everything is a dog'.

retractall(Head)

The predicate **retractall/1** takes a single argument which must be the head of a clause. It causes every clause in the database whose head matches *Head* to be deleted. The **retractall** goal always succeeds even if no clauses are deleted.

Some examples are:

?-retractall(mypred(_,_,_)).

which deletes all the clauses for the **mypred/3** predicate, and

?-retractall(parent(john,Y)).

which deletes all clauses for the **parent/2** predicate which have the atom *john* as their first argument.

Note that the query

?-retractall(mypred).

only removes the clauses for predicate **mypred/0**, i.e. the atom mypred. To delete all the clauses for predicate **mypred/3** it is necessary to use

?-retractall(mypred(_,_,_)).

with three anonymous variables.

8.4 Changing the Database: Example

The following example, which comprises a series of goals entered at the system prompt, illustrates the use of the **assertz, asserta, retract** and **retractall** predicates for changing the database.

```
?- assertz(mypred(first)).    Four mypred clauses are added to
                                  the database.
true.
?- assertz(mypred(second)).
true.
?- assertz(mypred(third)).
true.
?- assertz(mypred(fourth)).
true.
?- listing(mypred).           The four mypred clauses are now in
                                  the database.
```

```
/* mypred/1 */
mypred(first).
mypred(second).
mypred(third).
mypred(fourth).
true.
?- asserta(mypred(new1)).
true.

?- listing(mypred).
:- dynamic mypred/1.
mypred(new1).
mypred(first).
mypred(second).
mypred(third).
mypred(fourth).
true.

?- assertz(mypred(new2)).
true.

?- listing(mypred).
:- dynamic mypred/1.
mypred(new1).
mypred(first).
mypred(second).
mypred(third).
mypred(fourth).
mypred(new2).
true.
?- mypred(X).
X = new1 ;
X = first ;
X = second ;

X = third ;
X = fourth ;
X = new2
?- retract(mypred(first)).
true.

?- listing(mypred).
:- dynamic mypred/1.
mypred(new1).
mypred(second).
mypred(third).
mypred(fourth).
mypred(new2).
true.
```

A new mypred clause is added to the database, using the asserta predicate.

This shows that asserta places the new clause above the other mypred clauses in the database.

A message indicating that mypred/1 is dynamic is also displayed. Any predicate not already in the database that is created using assertz/1 or asserta/1 will automatically be treated as dynamic.

A further mypred clause is added to the database using the assertz predicate.

This shows that assertz places the new clause below the other mypred clauses in the database.

This shows that retrieving mypred clauses from the database will give the first one listed by the listing predicate.

Subsequent backtracking will obtain the remaining clauses in top to bottom order.

One of the mypred clauses is removed from the database using the retract predicate.

This shows that it has successfully been removed.

```
?- retractall(mypred(_)).        This is the correct way to remove all
true.                                 mypred clauses with one argument
                                      from the database.
?- listing(mypred).              This shows that all the
:- dynamic mypred/1.                  mypred clauses have
true.                                 been removed.
```

8.5   Maintaining a Database of Facts

The predicates **assertz, retract** etc. can be used to create and maintain a database
of related facts within the full Prolog database of facts and rules.

Creating a Database

Assume file people.txt contains the six lines

```
john. smith. 45. london. doctor.
martin. williams. 33. birmingham. teacher.
henry. smith. 26. manchester. plumber.
jane. wilson. 62. london. teacher.
mary. smith. 29. glasgow. surveyor.
end.
```

Assume also that there is a program file containing the following.

```
setup:-seeing(S),see('people.txt'),
  read_data,
  write('Data read'),nl,
  seen,see(S).
read_data:-
  read(A),process(A).
process(end).
process(A):-
  read(B),read(C),read(D),read(E),
  assertz(person(A,B,C,D,E)),read_data.
```

Consulting the program file and then entering the query

?-setup.

will cause the file people.txt to be read and five clauses such as

```
person(john,smith,45,london,doctor).
```

to be added to the Prolog database.

?- setup.
Data read
true.

The **listing** predicate can be used to show all the clauses defining the **person** predicate.

?- listing(person).
:- dynamic person/5.

person(john, smith, 45, london, doctor).
person(martin, williams, 33, birmingham, teacher).
person(henry, smith, 26, manchester, plumber).
person(jane, wilson, 62, london, teacher).
person(mary, smith, 29, glasgow, surveyor).
true.

The effect is almost the same as if the five **person** clauses had been included in the original program file. The only difference is that since the **person** clauses were not (directly) loaded from a program file using **consult** but were read in from a data file and entered into the database using the **assertz** predicate the system considers the predicate **person/5** to be dynamic not static.

Removing a Clause

Predicate **remove** will delete a single clause from the database.

```
remove(Forename,Surname):-
    retract(person(Forename,Surname,_,_,_)).
```

?- remove(henry,smith).
true.

?- listing(person).

:- dynamic person/5.

person(john, smith, 45, london, doctor).

person(martin, williams, 33, birmingham, teacher).
person(jane, wilson, 62, london, teacher).
person(mary, smith, 29, glasgow, surveyor).
true.

Changing a Clause

Predicate **change** will change a clause by retracting the old version and asserting a
new one.

change(Forename,Surname,New_Profession):-
person(Forename,Surname,Age,City,Profession),
retract(person(Forename,Surname,Age,City,Profession)),
assertz(person(Forename,Surname,Age,City,New_Profession)).

?- change(jane,wilson,architect).
true.

?- listing(person).

:- dynamic person/5.

person(john, smith, 45, london, doctor).
person(martin, williams, 33, birmingham, teacher).
person(mary, smith, 29, glasgow, surveyor).
person(jane, wilson, 62, london, architect).
true.

Outputting the Database to a File

Predicate **output_data** will write out the **person** clauses to a new file in the same
format as the original file.

```
output_data:-
    telling(T),tell('people2.txt'),
    write_data,told,tell(T),
    write('Data written'),nl.
write_data:-person(A,B,C,D,E),
    write(A),write('. '),
    write(B),write('. '),
```

```
    write(C),write('. '),
    write(D),write('. '),
    write(E),write('.'),nl,
    fail.
write_data:-write('end.'),nl.
```

?- output_data.
Data written

true.

creates file people2.txt

```
john. smith. 45. london. doctor.
martin. williams. 33. birmingham. teacher.
mary. smith. 29. glasgow. surveyor.
jane. wilson. 62. london. architect.
end.
```

Chapter Summary

This chapter describes the built-in predicates for adding clauses to or deleting
clauses from the Prolog database and shows how to use them to create and
maintain a database of related facts within the overall Prolog database.

Practical Exercise 8

(1) Define and test a predicate **add_data** which reads a series of names of animals
   (e.g. cat, dog, mouse) entered by the user, terminated by *end*. It should add a
   corresponding series of facts, e.g. **animal(dog)** to the Prolog database, ignoring
   any names that have already been entered.
(2) Define and test a predicate **display_animals** which lists the names of all the
   animals in the database, one per line.
(3) Define and test a predicate **remove2** which removes any clauses corresponding
   to either a dog or a cat from the database, if they are present, and otherwise has
   no effect.

Chapter 9
List Processing

Chapter Aims

After reading this chapter you should be able to:

- Represent data in the form of lists
- Use built-in predicates to manipulate lists
- Define predicates to work through a list element by element from left to right using recursion.

9.1 Representing Data as Lists

Prolog's compound terms give a flexible way of representing data, especially as the arguments may be other terms of any complexity. For example, the following is a valid term: **mypred(a,-6.3,pred2(p,pred3(3,q,aaa),r)).**

However, in common with most other programming languages, compound terms suffer from the limitation that each predicate must have a fixed number of arguments. It is possible to use **mypred** sometimes with three arguments and sometimes with four, say, but Prolog regards these as two entirely different predicates.

To overcome this limitation, Prolog provides a very flexible type of data object called a *list*. A list is written as a sequence of values, known as *list elements*, separated by commas and enclosed in square brackets, e.g. **[dog,cat,fish,man].**

A list element does not have to be an atom. It can be any Prolog term, including a bound or unbound variable or another list, so **[X,Y,mypred(a,b,c),[p,q,r],z]** is a valid list. A list element that is itself a list is known as a *sublist*.

Lists can have any number of elements, including zero. The list with no elements is known as the *empty list* and is written as **[]**.

For non-empty lists, the first element is known as the *head*. The list remaining after the first element is removed is called the *tail*. For example, the head of the list **[dog,cat,fish,man]** is the atom *dog* and the tail is the list **[cat,fish,man].**

M. Bramer, *Logic Programming with Prolog*, DOI 10.1007/978-1-4471-5487-7_9,
© Springer-Verlag London 2013

The head of list [x,y,mypred(a,b,c),[p,q,r],z] is the atom *x*. The tail is the list **[y,mypred(a,b,c),[p,q,r],z]**.

Some further examples of lists are:

[john,mary,10,robert,20,jane,X,bill]
[[john,28],[mary,56,teacher],robert,parent(victoria,albert),[a,b,[c,d,e],f],28]
[[portsmouth,london,glasgow],[portsmouth,london,edinburgh],[glasgow]]

9.2   Notation for Lists

Up to now lists have been written as a sequence of list elements written in order, separated by commas and enclosed in square brackets. We will call this 'standard bracketed notation'.

Lists are generally, although not always, written in this notation in queries entered by the user at the system prompt, for example

?- X=alpha,Y=27,Z=[alpha,beta],write('List is: '),write([X,Y,Z]),nl.
List is: [alpha,27,[alpha,beta]]

However (with the exception of the empty list) lists are seldom written in this way in a Prolog program. The explanation for this is that lists are most useful (and generally only used) when the programmer does not know in advance how many elements they will contain. If we know that a list will always contain three elements, say a person's forename, surname and nationality, it would generally be better to use a compound term with three arguments, such as **person(john, smith, british).**

Lists are most valuable when the number of elements needed cannot be known in advance and would probably vary from one use of the program to another. For example, we might want to define a predicate that reads in information about an organisation's purchases in a given financial year and writes out a list of all the items of computer hardware or software purchased in the months from March to June inclusive that cost more than a certain amount. In this case we would certainly not wish to build in any assumption that the list will always have fifteen or any other fixed number of elements. It might potentially be any number, from zero upwards.

We need an alternative way of representing a list in a Prolog clause that does not make any commitment to the number of elements it will have when the clause is used. This is provided by the 'cons' (standing for list constructor) notation.

In this notation a list is written in a more complicated form than before, with two parts joined together by the vertical bar character | which is known as the *cons character* or simply as *cons*. Thus a list is represented by the notation [*elements* | *list*].

The *elements* part is a sequence of one or more list elements, which may be any Prolog terms. The *list* part (obviously) represents a list.

The list **[elements | list]** is an augmented version of the list **list** with the sequence of elements indicated by **elements** inserted before any elements that are already there.

For example, [one|[two,three]] represents [one,two,three].

The following shows some equivalent ways of writing the same list of four elements. We will come on to lists of variable length after that.

[alpha,beta,gamma,delta]
[alpha|[beta,gamma,delta]]
[alpha,beta|[gamma,delta]]
[alpha,beta,gamma|[delta]]
[alpha,beta,gamma,delta|[]]
[alpha,beta|[gamma|[delta|[]]]]

The cons notation for a list can be used anywhere the 'standard bracketed form' would be valid, e.g.

?- write([alpha|[beta,gamma,delta]]),nl.
[alpha,beta,gamma,delta]
true.

?- write([alpha,beta,gamma|[delta]]),nl.
[alpha,beta,gamma,delta]
true.

?- write([alpha,beta,gamma,delta|[]]),nl.
[alpha,beta,gamma,delta]
true.

?- write([alpha,beta|[gamma,delta]]),nl.
[alpha,beta,gamma,delta]
true.

?- write([alpha,beta|[gamma|[delta|[]]]]),nl.
[alpha,beta,gamma,delta]
true.

In the common case where the *elements* part of **[elements | list]** consists of just one term, the 'cons' notation can be used to construct a list from its head and tail, which are the parts to the left and right of the vertical bar respectively. Thus **[a|[b,c,d]]** denotes the list **[a,b,c,d]**.

As illustrated so far, there would be no benefit gained by using the 'cons' notation rather than the standard bracketed notation. The former is of most value when the *list* part is a variable and/or the *elements* part contains one or more variables.

For example, if variable *L* is bound to a list, say **[red,blue,green,yellow]**, we can represent a new list with the atom **brown** inserted before the elements already there by **[brown|L]**.

?- L=[red,blue,green,yellow],write([brown|L]),nl.
[brown,red,blue,green,yellow]

If variable *A* is bound to the list **[brown,pink]** and variable *L* is bound to the list **[red,blue,green,yellow]**, the list **[A,A,black|L]** represents

[[brown,pink],[brown,pink],black,red,blue,green,yellow].

We are now in a position to write a clause or a query that makes use of a list without knowing in advance how many elements it will have. This example shows a new list *L1* created from a list *L* input by the user.

?- write('Type a list: '),read(L),L1=[start|L],write('New list is '),write(L1),nl.
Type a list: [[london,paris],[x,y,z],27].
New list is [start,[london,paris],[x,y,z],27]

The 'cons' notation for lists is so much more flexible than the standard bracketed notation that some would say that it is the 'correct' notation for lists, and that a list written in the standard bracketed notation, such as **[dog,cat,fish,man]** is just a more human-readable version of **[dog|[cat|[fish|[man|[]]]]]**.

9.3   Decomposing a List

A common requirement is to perform the same (or a similar) operation on every element of a list. By far the best way of processing a list is to work through its elements one by one from left to right. This can be achieved by breaking the list into its head and tail and processing each separately in a recursive fashion. Paradoxically, breaking a list into its head and tail is often done using the list constructor.

The predicate **writeall** defined below writes out the elements of a list, one per line.

The second clause of **writeall** separates a list into its head *A* and tail *L*, writes out *A* and then a newline, then calls itself again recursively. The first clause of **writeall** ensures that evaluation terminates when no further elements of the list remain to be output.

```
/* write out the elements of a list, one per line */
writeall([]).
writeall([A|L]):- write(A),nl,writeall(L).
```

?- writeall([alpha,'this is a string',20,[a,b,c]]).
alpha
this is a string
20
[a,b,c]
true.

This definition of **writeall** is typical of many user-defined predicates for list processing. Note that although **writeall** takes a list as its argument, its definition does not include a statement beginning

```
writeall(L):-
```

Instead, the main part of the definition begins

```
writeall([A|L]):-
```

This makes the definition of the predicate considerably easier.

When a goal such as **writeall([a,b,c])** is evaluated, it is matched against (unified with) the head of the second clause of **writeall.** As this is written as **writeall([A|L])** the matching process causes A to be bound to atom **a** and L to be bound to list **[b,c].** This makes it easy for the body of the rule to process the head and tail separately.

The recursive call to **writeall** with the tail of the original list, i.e. L, as its argument is a standard programming technique used in list processing. As is frequently the case, the empty list is treated separately, in this case by the first clause of **writeall.**

The predicate **write_english** defined below takes as its argument a list such as

**[[london,england],[paris,france],[berlin,germany],[portsmouth,england],
[bristol,england],[edinburgh,scotland]]**

Each element is a *sublist* containing the name of a city and the name of the country in which it is located. Calling **write_english** causes the names of all the cities that are located in England to be output.

The second clause of **write_english** deals with those sublists that have the atom *england* as their second element. In this case the first element is output, followed by a new line and a recursive call to **write_english,** with the tail of the original list as the argument. Sublists that do not have *england* as their second element are dealt with by the final clause of **write_english,** which does nothing with the sublist but makes a recursive call to **write_english,** with the tail of the original list as the argument.

```
write_english([]).
write_english([[City,england]|L]):-
  write(City),nl,
  write_english(L).
```

```
write_english([A|L]):-write_english(L).
go:- write_english([[london,england],[paris,france],
    [berlin,germany],[portsmouth,england],
    [bristol,england],
    [edinburgh,scotland]]).
```

?- go.
london
portsmouth
bristol
true.

The predicate **replace** defined below takes as its first argument a list of at least one element. If the second argument is an unbound variable, it is bound to the same list with the first element replaced by the atom **first**. Using the 'cons' notation, the definition takes only one clause.

```
replace([A|L],[first|L]).
```

?- replace([1,2,3,4,5],L).
L = [first,2,3,4,5]

?- replace([[a,b,c],[d,e,f],[g,h,i]],L).
L = [first, [d,e,f],[g,h,i]]

9.4 Built-in Predicate: member

The ability to represent data in the form of lists is such a valuable feature of Prolog that several built-in predicates have been provided for it. The most commonly used of these are described in this and the following sections.

The **member** built-in predicate takes two arguments. If the first argument is any term except a variable and the second argument is a list, **member** succeeds if the first argument is a member of the list denoted by the second argument (i.e. one of its list elements).

?- member(a,[a,b,c]).
true.

?- member(mypred(a,b,c),[q,r,s,mypred(a,b,c),w]).
true.

?- member(x,[]).
false.

?- member([1,2,3],[a,b,[1,2,3],c]).
true.

If the first argument is an unbound variable, it is bound to an element of the list working from left to right (thus if it is called only once it will be bound to the first element). This can be used in conjunction with backtracking to find all the elements of a list in turn from left to right, as follows.

?- member(X,[a,b,c]).
X = a ;
X = b ;
X = c ;
false.

Predicate **get_answer2** defined below reads a term entered by the user. It loops using **repeat,** until one of a list of permitted answers *(yes, no* or *maybe)* is entered and the **member** goal is satisfied.

```
get_answer2(Ans):-repeat,
  write('answer yes, no or maybe: '),read(Ans),
  member(Ans,[yes,no,maybe]),
  write('answer is '),write(Ans),nl,!.
```

?- get_answer2(X).
answer yes, no or maybe: possibly.
answer yes, no or maybe: unsure.
answer yes, no or maybe: maybe.
answer is maybe
X = maybe

9.5   Built-in Predicate: length

The **length** built-in predicate takes two arguments. The first is a list. If the second is an unbound variable it is bound to the length of the list, i.e. the number of elements it contains.

?- length([a,b,c,d],X).
X = 4
?- length([[a,b,c],[d,e,f],[g,h,i]],L).
L = 3
?- length([],L).
L = 0

If the second argument is a number, or a variable bound to a number, its value is compared with the length of the list.

?- length([a,b,c],3).
true.

?- length([a,b,c],4).
false.

?- N is 3,length([a,b,c],N).
N = 3

9.6   Built-in Predicate: reverse

The **reverse** built-in predicate takes two arguments. If the first is a list and the second is an unbound variable (or vice versa), the variable will be bound to the value of the list with the elements written in reverse order, e.g.

?- reverse([1,2,3,4],L).
L = [4,3,2,1]

?- reverse(L,[1,2,3,4]).
L = [4,3,2,1]

?- reverse([[dog,cat],[1,2],[bird,mouse],[3,4,5,6]],L).
L = [[3,4,5,6],[bird,mouse],[1,2],[dog,cat]]

Note that the order of the elements of the sublists **[dog,cat]** etc. is not reversed. If both arguments are lists, **reverse** succeeds if one is the reverse of the other.

?- reverse([1,2,3,4],[4,3,2,1]).
true.

?- reverse([1,2,3,4],[3,2,1]).
false.

The predicate **front/2** defined below takes a list as its first argument. If the second argument is an unbound variable it is bound to a list which is the same as the first list with the last element removed. For example if the first list is **[a,b,c]**, the second will be **[a,b]**. In the body of the rule the first list $L1$ is reversed to give $L3$. Its head is then removed to give $L4$ and $L4$ is then reversed back again to give $L2$.

```
front(L1,L2):-
    reverse(L1,L3),remove_head(L3,L4),reverse(L4,L2).
remove_head([A|L],L).
```

?- **front([a,b,c],L).**
L = [a,b]

?- **front([[a,b,c],[d,e,f],[g,h,i]],L).**
L = [[a,b,c],[d,e,f]]

The **front** predicate can also be used with two lists as arguments. In this case it tests whether the second list is the same as the first list with the last element removed.

?- **front([a,b,c],[a,b]).**
true.

?- **front([[a,b,c],[d,e,f],[g,h,i]],[[a,b,c],[d,e,f]]).**
true.

?- **front([a,b,c,d],[a,b,d]).**
false.

9.7 Built-in Predicate: append

The term *concatenating* two lists means creating a new list, the elements of which are those of the first list followed by those of the second list. Thus concatenating **[a,b,c]** with **[p,q,r,s]** gives the list **[a,b,c,p,q,r,s]**. Concatenating **[]** with **[x,y]** gives **[x,y]**.

The **append** built-in predicate takes three arguments. If the first two arguments are lists and the third argument is an unbound variable, the third argument is bound to a list comprising the first two lists concatenated, e.g.

?- **append([1,2,3,4],[5,6,7,8,9],L).**
L = [1,2,3,4,5,6,7,8,9]

?- **append([],[1,2,3],L).**
L = [1,2,3]

?- **append([[a,b,c],d,e,f],[g,h,[i,j,k]],L).**
L = [[a,b,c],d,e,f,g,h,[i,j,k]]

The **append** predicate can also be used in other ways. When the first two arguments are variables and the third is a list it can be used with backtracking to find all possible pairs of lists which when concatenated give the third argument, as follows.

?- **append(L1,L2,[1,2,3,4,5]).**
L1 = [] ,
L2 = [1,2,3,4,5] ;

L1 = [1] ,

L2 = [2,3,4,5] ;

L1 = [1,2] ,
L2 = [3,4,5] ;

L1 = [1,2,3] ,
L2 = [4,5] ;

L1 = [1,2,3,4] ,
L2 = [5] ;

L1 = [1,2,3,4,5] ,
L2 = [] ;
false.

This example shows a list broken up in a more complex way.

?- append(X,[Y|Z],[1,2,3,4,5,6]).
X = [] ,
Y = 1 ,
Z = [2,3,4,5,6] ;

X = [1] ,
Y = 2 ,
Z = [3,4,5,6] ;

X = [1,2] ,
Y = 3 ,
Z = [4,5,6] ;

X = [1,2,3] ,
Y = 4 ,
Z = [5,6] ;

X = [1,2,3,4] ,
Y = 5 ,
Z = [6] ;

X = [1,2,3,4,5] ,
Y = 6 ,
Z = [] ;

false.

9.8   List Processing: Examples

This section shows some examples of list processing, all of which illustrate the use of recursion.

Example 1

The predicate **find_largest/2** takes a list of numbers as its first argument and assigns the value of the largest element to its second argument (assumed to be an unbound variable). It is assumed that the list contains at least one number.

```
find_largest([X|List],Maxval):-
find_biggest(List,Maxval,X).
find_biggest([],Currentlargest,Currentlargest).
find_biggest([A|L],Maxval,Currentlargest):-
  A>Currentlargest,
  find_biggest(L,Maxval,A).
find_biggest([A|L],Maxval,Currentlargest):-
  A=<Currentlargest,
  find_biggest(L,Maxval,Currentlargest).
```

Calling the **find_largest** goal with the list of numbers as its first argument causes the first element of the list to be removed and passed to **find_biggest** as its third argument (the largest number found so far). The remainder of the list is passed to **find_biggest** as its first argument (a list of the numbers not yet examined). The second argument of **find_largest** (Maxval) represents the overall largest number and is unbound because the value is not yet known. It is passed to **find_biggest** as its second argument.

The three arguments of **find-biggest/3** represent in order:

- the list of numbers not so far examined
- the overall largest number (to be passed back to **find_largest**)
- the largest number found so far.

So the first clause of **find_biggest** can be read as: 'if there are no more numbers remaining unexamined, return the largest number so far (third argument) as the value of the overall largest number (second argument)'. The second argument becomes bound.

The second clause of **find_biggest** can be read as: 'if the list of numbers so far not examined begins with value A and A is larger than the largest so far found, call **find_biggest** (recursively) with L, the tail of the (first argument) list, as the new first argument (list of unexamined numbers) and with A as the third argument (largest number so far)'. The second argument (Maxval) is unbound.

The final clause of **find_biggest** can be read as: 'if the list of numbers so far not examined begins with value A and A is not larger than the largest so far found, call **find_biggest** (recursively) with L, the tail of the (first argument) list, as the new first argument (list of unexamined numbers) and with the third argument (largest number so far) unchanged'. The second argument (Maxval) is unbound.

?- find_largest([10,20,678,-4,-12,102,-5],M).
M = 678

?- find_largest([30,10],M).
M = 30

?- find_largest([234],M).
M = 234

Example 2

The **front/2** predicate was defined in Section 9.6 as an example of the use of the **reverse** built-in predicate. It takes a list as its first argument. If the second argument is an unbound variable it is bound to a list which is the same as the first list with the last element removed. For example if the first list is **[a,b,c]**, the second will be **[a,b]**.
The predicate can be defined more efficiently using recursion as follows.

```
front([X],[]).
front([X|Y],[X|Z]):-front(Y,Z).
```

The two clauses can be read as 'the front of a list with just one element is the empty list' and 'the front of a list with head X and tail Y is the list with head X and tail Z where Z is the front of Y', respectively.

?- front([alpha],L).
L = []

?- front([alpha,beta,gamma],LL).
LL = [alpha,beta]

?- front([[a,b],[c,d,e],[f,g,h]],L1).
L1 = [[a,b],[c,d,e]]

Example 3

One area in which different Prolog implementations can vary considerably is the provision of built-in predicates for list processing. If your implementation does not have **member/2, reverse/2** or **append/3** (described in Sections 9.4, 9.6 and 9.7 respectively) you can define your own with just a few clauses as shown below.

```
member(X,[X|L]).
member(X,[_|L]):-member(X,L).
reverse(L1,L2):-rev(L1,[],L2).
rev([],L,L).
```

```
rev([A|L],L1,L2):-rev(L,[A|L1],L2).
append([],L,L).
append([A|L1],L2,[A|L3]):-append(L1,L2,L3).
```

The two clauses defining **member/2** just state that X is a member of any list with head X (i.e. that begins with X) and that X is a member of any list for which it is not the head if it is a member of the tail.

The definitions of the other two predicates are slightly more complex and are left without explanation.

If your implementation of Prolog has any or all these predicates built-in, it is still possible to test the definitions above by renaming the predicates systematically as **mymember, myreverse** and **myappend,** say, giving the following program.

```
mymember(X,[X|L]).
mymember(X,[_|L]):-mymember(X,L).
myreverse(L1,L2):-rev(L1,[],L2).
rev([],L,L).
rev([A|L],L1,L2):-rev(L,[A|L1],L2).
myappend([],L,L).
myappend([A|L1],L2,[A|L3]):-myappend(L1,L2,L3).
```

This can then be tested using some of the examples in Sections 9.4, 9.6 and 9.7, for which it gives the same results in each case.

?- mymember(X,[a,b,c]).
X = a ;
X = b ;
X = c ;
false.

?- mymember(mypred(a,b,c),[q,r,s,mypred(a,b,c),w]).
true.

?- mymember(x,[]).
false.

?- myreverse([1,2,3,4],L).
L = [4,3,2,1]

?- myreverse([[dog,cat],[1,2],[bird,mouse],[3,4,5,6]],L).
L = [[3,4,5,6],[bird,mouse],[1,2],[dog,cat]]

?- **myappend([1,2,3,4],[5,6,7,8,9],L).**
L = [1,2,3,4,5,6,7,8,9]

?- **myappend([],[1,2,3],L).**
L = [1,2,3]

9.9 Using findall/3 to Create a List

It would often be desirable to find all the values that would satisfy a goal, not just
one of them. The **findall/3** predicate provides a powerful facility for creating lists
of all such values. It is particularly useful when used in conjunction with the Prolog
database.

If the database contains the five clauses

```
person(john,smith,45,london).
person(mary,jones,28,edinburgh).
person(michael,wilson,62,bristol).
person(mark,smith,37,cardiff).
person(henry,roberts,23,london).
```

a list of all the surnames (the second argument of **person**) can be obtained using
findall by entering the goal:

?- **findall(S,person(_,S,_,_),L).**

This returns

L = [smith,jones,wilson,smith,roberts]

L is a list of all the values of variable *S* which satisfy the goal **person(_,S,_,_)**.
The predicate **findall/3** has three arguments. The first is generally an unbound
variable, but can be any term with at least one unbound variable as an argument (or
equivalently any list with at least one unbound variable as a list element).

The second argument must be a goal, i.e. must be in a form that could appear on
the right-hand side of a rule or be entered at the system prompt.

The third argument should be an unbound variable. Evaluating **findall** will cause
this to be bound to a list of all the possible values of the term (first argument) that
satisfy the goal (second argument).

More complex lists can be constructed by making the first argument a term
involving several variables, rather than using a single variable. For example

?- **findall([Forename,Surname],person(Forename,Surname,_,_),L).**

returns the list

L = [[john,smith],[mary,jones],[michael,wilson],[mark,smith],[henry,roberts]]

The term (first argument) can be embellished further, e.g.

?- findall([londoner,A,B],person(A,B,_,london),L).

returns the list

L = [[londoner,john,smith],[londoner,henry,roberts]]

Given a database containing clauses such as

```
age(john,45).
age(mary,28).
age(michael,62).
age(henry,23).
age(george,62).
age(bill,17).
age(martin,62).
```

the predicate **oldest_list/1** defined below can be used to create a list of the names of the oldest people in the database (in this case michael, george and martin, who are all 62).

It begins by calling **findall** to find the ages of all the people in the database and put them in a list *Agelist.*

It then uses the predicate **find_largest** (defined previously) to find the largest of these values and bind variable *Oldest* to that value. Finally, it uses **findall** again to create a list of the names of all the people of that age.

```
oldest_list(L):-
   findall(A,age(_,A),Agelist),
   find_largest(Agelist,Oldest),
   findall(Name,age(Name,Oldest),L).
```

?- oldest_list(L).
L = [michael,george,martin]

The final example in this section shows a predicate **find_under_30s** used in conjunction with the **age** predicate from the previous example to create a list of the names of all those people under 30. This requires only one new clause.

```
find_under_30s(L):-findall(Name,(age(Name,A),A<30),L).
```

?- find_under_30s(L).
L = [mary,henry,bill]

The second argument of **findall** is the goal **(age(Name,A),A<30)**. It is important to place parentheses around it so that it is treated as a single (compound) goal with two component subgoals, not as two goals. Omitting the parentheses would give a predicate named **findall** with four arguments. This would be an entirely different predicate from **findall/3** and one unknown to the Prolog system.

Chapter Summary

This chapter describes a flexible type of data object called a list. It shows how to work through a list element by element from left to right using recursion to perform the same or a similar operation on each element, how to manipulate lists using built-in predicates and how to create a list containing all the possible values that would satisfy a specified goal.

Practical Exercise 9

(1) Define and test a predicate **pred1** that takes a list as its first argument and returns the tail of the list as its second argument, e.g.

?- pred1([a,b,c],L).
L = [b,c]

(2) Define and test a predicate **inc** that takes a list of numbers as its first argument and returns a list of the same numbers all increased by one as its second argument, e.g.

?- inc([10,20,-7,0],L).
L = [11,21,-6,1]

(3) Define and test a predicate **palindrome** that checks whether a list reads the same way forwards and backwards, e.g.

?- palindrome([a,b,c,b,a]).
true.

?- palindrome([a,b,c,d,e]).
false.

(4) Define and test a predicate **putfirst** that adds a specified term to the beginning of a list, e.g.

?- putfirst(a,[b,c,d,e],L).
L = [a,b,c,d,e]

(5) Define and test a predicate **putlast** that adds a specified term to the end of a list, e.g.

?- putlast(e,[a,b,c,d],L).
L = [a,b,c,d,e]

(6) Using **findall** define and test predicates **pred2/2, pred3/2** and **pred4/2** that modify a list, as shown in the following examples:

?- pred2([a,b,c,d,e],L).
L = [[a],[b],[c],[d],[e]]

?- pred3([a,b,c,d,e],L).
L = [pred(a,a),pred(b,b),pred(c,c),pred(d,d),pred(e,e)]

?- pred4([a,b,c,d,e],L).
L = [[element,a],[element,b],[element,c],[element,d],[element,e]]

Chapter 10
String Processing

Chapter Aims

After reading this chapter you should be able to:

- Use a built-in predicate to convert strings of characters to lists and vice versa
- Define predicates for the most common types of string processing.

10.1 Converting Strings of Characters To and From Lists

An atom such as 'hello world' can be regarded as a string of characters. Prolog has facilities to enable strings of this kind to be manipulated, e.g.

- To join two strings such as 'Today is' and 'Tuesday' to form 'Today is Tuesday'.
- To remove initial spaces, e.g. to replace '   hello world' by 'hello world'.
- To find the part of the string after (or before) a specified string, e.g. to find the name in a string such as 'My name is John Smith'.

Prolog does this by converting strings to equivalent lists of numbers using the **name/2** predicate and then using list processing techniques such as those discussed in Chapter 9, before (generally) converting the resulting lists back to strings.

The **name/2** predicate takes two arguments. If the first is an atom and the second is an unbound variable, evaluating a **name** goal will cause the variable to be bound to a list of numbers equivalent to the string of characters that forms the atom, for example:

?- name('Prolog Example',L).
L = [80,114,111,108,111,103,32,69,120,97,109,112,108,101]

As discussed in Chapter 5, each of the 256 possible characters has an equivalent ASCII (American Standard Code for Information Interchange) value, which is an integer from 0 to 255 inclusive.

M. Bramer, *Logic Programming with Prolog*, DOI 10.1007/978-1-4471-5487-7_10,
© Springer-Verlag London 2013

9	tab	40	(	59	;	94	∧
10	end of record	41	)	60	<	95	_
32	space	42	*	61	=	96	`
33	!	43	+	62	>	97–122	a to z
34	"	44	,	63	?		
35	#	45	-	64	@	123	{
36	$	46	.	65-90	A to Z	124	|
37	%	47	/	91	[	125	}
38	&	48-57	0 to 9	92	\	126	~
39	'	58	:	93	]		

The table of ASCII values corresponding to the most commonly used characters is reproduced here for convenience.

In the example above, 80 is the ASCII value corresponding to the character P, 114 corresponds to r etc., so the list

[80,114,111,108,111,103,32,69,120,97,109,112,108,101]

corresponds to 'Prolog Example'.

The **name** predicate can also be used to perform the conversion in the other direction, i.e. from a list of ASCII values to an equivalent atom.

?-name(A,[80,114,111,108,111,103,32,69,120,97,109,112,108,101]).
A = 'Prolog Example'

Once a string has been converted to list form it can be manipulated using any of the facilities available for list processing to produce a new list or lists, which can then be converted back to strings, again using the **name** predicate.

The examples in the following sections illustrate some of the programming techniques involved in processing strings.

10.2   Joining Two Strings

The predicate **join2/3** defined below shows how to join two strings (the first two arguments) to create a third string combining the two. The programming technique used is a typical one in string processing: convert both strings to lists, concatenate them using **append** and finally convert back the resulting list to a string.

```
/* Join two strings String1 and String2 to form a
new string Newstring */
join2(String1,String2,Newstring):-
  name(String1,L1),name(String2,L2),
  append(L1,L2,Newlist),
  name(Newstring,Newlist).
```

?- join2('prolog','example',S).
S = 'prolog example'

?- join2('','Prolog',S).
S = 'Prolog'

?- join2('Prolog','',S).
S = 'Prolog'

The predicate **join3/4** defined below uses **join2** twice to join three strings together.

```
/* Join three strings using the join2 predicate */
join3(String1,String2,String3,Newstring):-
    join2(String1,String2,S),
    join2(S,String3,Newstring).
```

?- join3('This is',' an',' example',Newstring).
Newstring = 'This is an example'

10.3   Trimming a String

This example shows how to define a predicate that will 'trim' a string, i.e. remove any white space characters (spaces, tabs etc.) at the beginning or end. This will be done in four stages.

Stage 1

Define and test a predicate **trim/2** which takes a list of integers as its first argument and an unbound variable as its second and binds the variable to the list with any elements less than or equal to 32 at the left-hand end removed. This makes use of the techniques described in Section 9.3, where the elements of a list are extracted one by one using *cons*.

```
trim([A|L],L1):-A=<32,trim(L,L1).
trim([A|L],[A|L]):-A>32.
```

?- trim([26,32,17,45,18,27,94,18,16,9],X).
X = [45,18,27,94,18,16,9]

Stage 2

Define and test a predicate **trim2/2** which takes a list of integers as its first argument and an unbound variable as its second and binds the variable to the list with any elements less than or equal to 32 at the right-hand end removed. This uses **trim** in conjunction with the **reverse** predicate.

```
trim2(L,L1):-
reverse(L,Lrev),trim(Lrev,L2),reverse(L2,L1).
```

?- trim2([45,18,27,94,18,16,9],X).
X = [45,18,27,94]

Stage 3

Define and test a predicate **trim3/2** which takes a list of integers as its first argument and an unbound variable as its second and binds the variable to the list with any elements less than or equal to 32 at the beginning and/or the end removed. This uses **trim** to deal with the beginning of the list and **trim2** to deal with the end.

```
trim3(L,L1):-trim(L,L2),trim2(L2,L1).
```

?- trim3([26,32,17,45,18,27,94,18,16,9],X).
X = [45,18,27,94]

Stage 4

Define and test a predicate **trims/2** which takes an atom as its first argument and an unbound variable as its second and binds the variable to the atom with any white space characters at the beginning or end removed. Now that the list processing predicates **trim, trim2** and **trim3** have been defined, **trims** only needs a one clause definition.

```
trims(S,Snew):-name(S,L),trim3(L,L1),name(Snew,L1).
```

?- trims('   hello world   ',X).
X = 'hello world'

10.4 Inputting a String of Characters

A very common requirement is to read an entire line of input either from the user's terminal or from a text file. The Prolog built-in predicates for input are rather limited. The **read/1** predicate will only read a single term, terminated by a full stop. The **get0/1** and **get/1** predicates will only read a single character.

The predicate **readline/1** defined below takes an unbound variable as its argument. Calling the predicate causes a line of input to be read from the user's terminal and the variable to be bound to an atom comprising all the characters read in, up to but not including a new line character (ASCII value 10).

Assume that the input is terminated by a character with ASCII value 10, which is not included in the atom created.

```
readline(S):-readline1([],L),name(S,L),!.
readline1(Oldlist,L):-get0(X),process(Oldlist,X,L).
process(Oldlist,10,Oldlist).
process(Oldlist,X,L):-
append(Oldlist,[X],L1),readline1(L1,L).
```

?- readline(S).
: abcdefg
S = abcdefg

?- readline(S).
: this is an example „.+-*/#@ - Note no quotes needed and no final full stop
S = ' this is an example „.+-*/#@ - Note no quotes needed and no final full stop'

The predicate **readlineF/2** defined below is adapted from **readline/1** to deal with input taken from a text file. It is assumed that the end of each record is signified by a character with ASCII Value 10.

```
/* readline adapted for input from text files */
readlineF(File,S):-
    see(File),readline1([],L),name(S,L),!,seen.
```

If text file *file1.txt* contains the following four lines

```
This is an example of
a text file with four lines -
each is terminated by an invisible character
with ASCII value 10
```

calling **readfileF** with first argument '*file1.txt*' will cause the first line of the file to be output.

?- readlineF('file1.txt',S).
S = 'This is an example of '

10.5   Searching a String

The predicate **separate/3** defined below separates a list L into those elements before and after the element 32.

```
separate(L,Before,After):-
  append(Before,[32|After],L),!.
```

It does this using **append** with the second argument a list with head 32 – another example of the value of using the *cons* notation to deconstruct a list.

?- separate([26,42,32,18,56,32,19,24],Before,After).
Before = [26,42] ,
After = [18,56,32,19,24]

?- separate([32,24,86],Before,After).
Before = [] ,
After = [24,86]

?- separate([24,86,32],Before,After).
Before = [24,86] ,
After = []

?- separate([24,98,45,72],Before,After).
false.

Predicate **splitup/1** defined below starts by converting a string S to a list L, then calls predicate **findnext/1,** which calls predicate **proc/2** in a recursive fashion to isolate the parts before and after each 32 element (corresponding to a space character) in turn, convert it to a string and write it on a separate line.

```
separate(L,Before,After):-
append(Before,[32|After],L),!.

findnext(L):-
separate(L,Before,After),proc(Before,After).
```

```
findnext (L) :-write ('Last item is '),
name (S,L) ,write (S) ,nl.

proc (Before,After) :-write ('Next item is '),
name (S,Before) ,write (S) ,nl,findnext (After) .

splitup (S) :-name (S,L) , findnext (L) .
```

?- splitup('The time has come the walrus said').
Next item is The
Next item is time
Next item is has
Next item is come
Next item is the
Next item is walrus
Last item is said
true.

The predicate **checkprolog/1,** which takes an unbound variable as its argument, causes a string of characters to be read from the user's terminal and the argument to be bound to either the atom *present* or the atom *absent,* depending on whether or not the input string includes the word *Prolog.*

The main predicate defined here is **startList/2,** which uses **append** to check whether all the elements in list *L1* appear at the beginning of list *L2.*

```
/* Uses predicate readline as defined previously */
startList (L1,L2) :-append (L1,X,L2) .

includedList (L1, []) :-!,fail.
includedList (L1,L2) :-startList (L1,L2) .
includedList (L1, [A|L2] ) :-includedList (L1,L2) .

checkit (L,Plist,present) :-includedList (Plist,L) .
checkit (_,_,absent) .

checkprolog (X) :-readline (S) ,name (S,L) ,
  name ('Prolog',Plist) ,checkit (L,Plist,X) , !.
```

?- checkprolog(X).
: Logic Programming with Prolog
X = present

?- checkprolog(X).
: Mercury Venus Earth Mars Jupiter Saturn Uranus Neptune Pluto
X = absent

10.6   Dividing a String into Its Component Parts

The predicate **splits/4** divides a string into the substrings to the left and right of another string called a *separator*. Its arguments correspond to the string, the separator, the left part and the right part in turn. For example:

?- splits('In the beginning was the word','the',Left,Right).
Left = 'In ' ,
Right = ' beginning was the word'

?- splits('my name is John Smith','is',Left,Right).
Left = 'my name ' ,
Right = ' John Smith'

The definition of this predicate is quite complex. There are four special cases.

(1) The separator appears more than once in the string. As can be seen from the first example above, the first (i.e. 'leftmost') occurrence is taken.
(2) The string begins with the separator. In this case the left part should be set to the separator and the right part should be set to the remainder of the string.
(3) The string ends with the separator. In this case the right part should be set to the separator and the left part should be set to the remainder of the string.
(4) The separator does not appear in the string. In this case the left part should be set to the string and the right part should be set to ".

The full definition is given below, followed by examples showing that cases (2), (3) and (4) are dealt with correctly.

```
splits(S,Separator,Separator,R):-
  name(Separator,L1),name(S,L3),
  append(L1,L2,L3),name(R,L2),!.
splits(S,Separator,L,Separator):-
  name(Separator,L2),name(S,L3),
  append(L1,L2,L3),name(L,L1),!.
splits(S,Separator,Left,Right):-
  name(S,L3),append(Lleft,Lrest,L3),
  name(Separator,L4),append(L4,Lright,Lrest),
  name(Left,Lleft),name(Right,Lright),!.
splits(S,_,S,"):-!.
```

?- splits('my name is John Smith','my name is ',Left,Right).
Left = 'my name is ' ,
Right = 'John Smith'

?- splits('my name is John Smith','John Smith',Left,Right).
Left = 'my name is ' ,
Right = 'John Smith'

?-splits('my name is my name is John Smith','is',Left,Right).
Left = 'my name ' ,
Right = ' my name is John Smith'

?- splits('my name is John Smith','Bill Smith',Left, Right).
Left = 'my name is John Smith' ,
Right = ''

Predicate **remove_spaces/2** defined below uses predicate **splits/4** to remove any initial spaces from a string. The key idea is to split the string using a string containing a space, i.e. ' ', as the separator. If the left part becomes bound to ' ' it implies that case (2) above has occurred, i.e. the string must have begun with the separator. In this case (first clause of **remove2**), the remainder of the string (the right part) is used and any further spaces are removed from it in the same way. If not, the final string is the same as the original string (second clause of **remove2**).

```
remove_spaces(S,S1):-
   splits(S,' ',Sleft,Sright),
   remove2(S,Sleft,Sright,S1),!.
remove2(S,' ',Sright,S1):-remove_spaces(Sright,S1).
remove2(S,_,_,S).
```

?- remove_spaces('hello world',X).
X = 'hello world'

?- remove_spaces('   hello world',X).
X = 'hello world'

Chapter Summary

This chapter describes the principal techniques of string processing in Prolog, based on converting from atoms to lists and vice versa. The techniques are illustrated with examples of user-defined predicates to meet common string processing requirements.

Practical Exercise 10

(1) Define and test a predicate **spalindrome** to check whether a string is a palindrome, e.g.

?- spalindrome('abcd dcba').

yes

?- spalindrome('xyz').

no

(2) Use the **name** predicate to define and test a predicate **remove_final** that removes any final spaces from a string, e.g.

?- remove_final('hello world   ',X).
X = 'hello world'

?- remove_final('hello world',X).
X = 'hello world'

(3) Define and test a predicate **replace** to replace the first character in a string by the character **?** (which has ASCII value 63), e.g.

?- replace('abcde',X).
X = '?bcde'

Chapter 11
More Advanced Features

Chapter Aims

After reading this chapter you should be able to:

- Define operators to extend the basic Prolog language
- Define basic operations on sets as well as numbers and strings
- Use built-in predicates to manipulate terms.

11.1   Introduction

This chapter looks at some of the more advanced features provided by Prolog: the use of operators to extend the language (e.g. to provide new arithmetic operators, improved facilities for processing strings or facilities for processing sets) and facilities for processing terms, converting them to lists or evaluating them as goals.

11.2   Extending Prolog: Arithmetic

Although Prolog allows the standard arithmetic operators (such as $+ - *$ and $/$) to be used in arithmetic expressions, there is no similar convenient notation for calculating factorials or to perform other less common but sometimes useful operations such as adding the squares of two numbers.

The built-in predicate **is/2** is used for evaluating arithmetic expressions. It is not permitted for the Prolog programmer to redefine this by adding new operators (or by any other means) and any attempt to do so would lead to a system error. However, by using the technique described in this section the programmer can get the same effect, so that expressions involving new arithmetic operators such as 6! are permitted or even so that the definitions of standard operators such as $+$ and $-$ are changed.

M. Bramer, *Logic Programming with Prolog*, DOI 10.1007/978-1-4471-5487-7_11,
© Springer-Verlag London 2013

The key to this is to define a replacement for the **is/2** operator. This new operator will be called **iss/2.** There are two steps involved.

Step 1: Define **iss/2** to be an operator

This can be done by entering the goal

?- op(700,xfx,iss).

at the system prompt or as a directive at the beginning of a program.

The third argument of the **op/3** goal is of course the name of the operator. The first argument is called its precedence. The second argument takes the rather strange form **xfx,** denoting that **iss** is an infix operator, which takes two arguments and will be written between them.

Step 2: Define the **iss/2** operator

The simplest definition of **iss/2** would be

```
?- op(700,xfx,iss).

X iss Y:-X is Y.
```

(The **op** directive has been included in the program file.)

This would simply make the operator **iss** equivalent to the built-in operator **is,** so for example:

?- Z iss 6+sqrt(25)−2.
Z = 9.0

This very simple definition would obviously not achieve much. An improved (but not yet ideal) attempt at defining **iss** is as follows. The effect of using **iss** in combination with the different types of arithmetic operator (+ − * / etc.) is specified explicitly in the first eight clauses. All other cases (e.g. expressions involving **sqrt, sin** etc.) are dealt with by the final clause. With these definitions the operator **iss** still has the same effect as **is.**

```
?- op(700,xfx,iss).

Y iss A+B:-Y is A+B,!.
Y iss A−B:-Y is A−B,!.
Y iss A*B:-Y is A*B,!.
Y iss A/B:-Y is A/B,!.
Y iss A//B:-Y is A//B,!.
Y iss A^B:-Y is A^B,!.
Y iss +A:-Y is A,!.
Y iss −A:-Y is −A,!.
Y iss X:- Y is X,!.
```

?- Y iss 6+4*3−2.
Y = 16

?- X iss 3,Y iss X+5.6−3*10+100.5.
X = 3 ,
Y = 79.1

?-Y iss (8+4)/3−(6*7).
Y = −38

?- A=3,B=4,Y iss sqrt(A*A+B*B).
A = 3 ,
B = 4 ,
Y = 5.0

?- Y iss 6+sqrt(25).
Y = 11.0

?- Y iss 6+sqrt(10+15).
Y = 11.0

Defining! as a Factorial Operator

Starting from this more elaborate definition of **iss,** we can now add further operators.

The mathematical function *factorial* is defined only for integer arguments. The value of 'factorial 6' is $6 \times 5 \times 4 \times 3 \times 2 \times 1$ and is written as 6! (i.e. the number 6 followed by an exclamation mark).

In general the value of N! is Nx(N−1)!. This leads to a two-line recursive definition of a predicate **factorial/2:**

```
factorial(1,1):-!.
factorial(N,Y):-N1 is N−1,factorial(N1,Y1),
    Y is N*Y1.
```

It is assumed that the first argument will always be an integer or a variable bound to an integer and the second argument is an unbound variable. Then, for example, the product $6 \times 5 \times 4 \times 3 \times 2 \times 1$ can be found by

?- factorial(6,Y).
Y = 720

This predicate can now be used to define a new arithmetic operator ! which will enable terms such as 6! or N! to be written when evaluating an arithmetic expression using the **iss** predicate. As usual, there are two actions required to do this.

Step 1: Define ! to be an operator

This can be done by entering the goal

?- op(150,xf,!).

The atom **xf** denotes that **!** is a postfix operator, which will appear after its argument, e.g. 6!. Its precedence is 150.

Step 2: Define the ! predicate

Using the definition of the factorial predicate already given, the **!** operator (or rather its effect when used together with the **iss** operator) can be defined by adding the following clause to the definition of **iss,** say as the first line.

```
Y iss N!:-N1 iss N,factorial(N1,Y),!.
```

This allows the exclamation mark character to be used in a convenient way to represent factorials.

?- Y iss 6!.
Y = 720

?- Y iss (3+2)!.
Y = 120

However, there is a flaw in the definition of **iss.** Entering a goal such as

?- Y iss 5!+6!.

will cause Prolog to crash with an error message such as 'Function Not Defined'.

The reason is that to evaluate this expression, Prolog makes use of the definition of the + operator, which is

```
Y iss A+B:-Y is A+B,!.
```

This causes it to try to evaluate the goal

Y is 5!+6!

which causes an error as in this context **5!** and **6!** are not numbers. They have no meaning at all outside their definition for the **iss** predicate.

The most satisfactory way of dealing with this problem is to modify the definition of the **iss** operator so that its arguments are themselves evaluated using **iss** before adding, multiplying etc. their values. This requires every clause in the definition of **iss/2** to be modified, expect for the last, and gives the following revised program.

```
?- op(700,xfx,iss).
?- op(150,xf,!).
factorial(1,1):-!.
factorial(N,Y):-N1 is N-1,factorial(N1,Y1),Y is N*Y1.
Y iss N!:-N1 iss N,factorial(N1,Y),!.
Y iss A+B :-A1 iss A,B1 iss B,Y is A1+B1,!.
Y iss A-B :-A1 iss A,B1 iss B,Y is A1-B1,!.
Y iss A*B :-A1 iss A,B1 iss B,Y is A1*B1,!.
Y iss A/B :-A1 iss A,B1 iss B,Y is A1/B1,!.
Y iss A//B :-A1 iss A,B1 iss B,Y is A1//B1,!.
Y iss A^B :-A1 iss A,B1 iss B,Y is A1^B1,!.
Y iss +A :-Y iss A,!.
Y iss -A :- A1 iss A,Y is -A1,!.
Y iss X :- Y is X,!.
```

With the new definition of the $+$ operator, if either of its arguments is an expression such as 5! it is converted to a number before it is used. If an argument is a number, it is 'converted' to itself by the final clause.

The ! operator now works as expected. When the goal **Y iss 5!+6!** is evaluated, the system first applies **iss** to **5!** and to **6!** producing the numbers 120 and 720, respectively, and then adds them together.

?-Y iss 6!.
Y = 720

?-Y iss (3+2)!.
Y= 120

?- Y iss 5!+6!.
Y = 840

?- Y iss 4+2,Z iss Y!+3!−4!.
Y = 6 ,
Z = 702

?- Y iss (3!)!.
Y = 720

?- Y iss −(3!).
Y = −6

Note that the above definition of **iss** is still not watertight. Expressions such as **sqrt(3!)** will cause the system to crash. This can be overcome by adding additional clauses such as

```
Y iss sqrt(A):-A1 iss A, Y is sqrt(A1),!.
```

for all the arithmetic functions, such as **sqrt, abs** and **sin** with which it is intended to use the new operator.

Defining ** as a Sum of Squares Operator

As well as factorial, we can define new operators that perform any operations we wish. For example we might want to have an infix operator ****** that returns the sum of the squares of its two arguments. This can be defined as follows.

Step 1: Define ** to be an operator

This can be done by entering the goal

?- op(120,yfx,**).

This specifies that ****** is an infix operator, which will appear between its two arguments, e.g. 3**4. Its precedence is 120.

Step 2: Define the ** operator

The ****** operator can be defined by adding the following clause to the definition of **iss,** anywhere except the final line (which is a 'catch all').

```
Y iss A**B:- A1 iss A, B1 iss B, Y is A1*A1+B1*B1,!.
```

?- Y iss 3**2.
Y = 13

?- Y iss (3**2)+2.
Y = 15

?- Y iss 6+3**4+8+1**2−10.
Y = 34

?- Y iss (3**1)**(2**1).
Y = 125

?- Y iss (3!)**(4!).
Y = 612.

Redefining Addition and Subtraction

Now that we have the **iss** predicate we can even use it to 'redefine' addition and subtraction if we wish. If we change the following clauses in the definition of **iss**

```
Y iss A+B:- A1 iss A,B1 iss B,Y is A1+B1,!.
Y iss A-B:- A1 iss A,B1 iss B,Y is A1-B1,!.
```

to

```
Y iss A+B:- A1 iss A,B1 iss B,Y is A1-B1,!.
Y iss A-B:- A1 iss A,B1 iss B,Y is A1+B1,!.
```

The effect will be to cause + to subtract and − to add. For example

?- Y iss 6+4.
Y = 2

?- Y iss 6−4.
Y = 10

11.3 Extending Prolog: Operations on Strings

Now that we have this useful predicate **iss/2** we do not have to restrict its use to numbers. The **join2/3** predicate was defined in Chapter 10. It takes three arguments, the first two of which are atoms (or variables bound to atoms). These atoms are regarded as strings.

Assuming the third argument is an unbound variable, evaluating a **join2** goal will cause it to be bound to another atom, which is the first two joined together.

For reference, the definition of the **join2** predicate and some examples of its use are repeated below.

```
/* Join two strings String1 and String2 to form a new
string Newstring */
join2(String1,String2,Newstring):-
    name(String1,L1),name(String2,L2),
    append(L1,L2,Newlist),
    name(Newstring,Newlist).
```

?- join2('prolog',' example',S).
S = 'prolog example'

?- join2('','Prolog',S).
S = 'Prolog'

?- join2('Prolog','',S).
S = 'Prolog'

Although this is fine as far as it goes, it would be more convenient to be able to use an operator such as ++ to join two strings. This can be achieved by first defining the operator, by entering a goal such as

?- op(200,yfx,++).

and then adding the following clause to the definition of the **iss** predicate:

```
S iss S1++S2:-join2(S1,S2,S),!.
```

?- S iss 'hello'++' world'.
S = 'hello world'

Joining more than two strings together using ++ encounters problems similar to those in the last section. Evaluating the sequence of goals

?- X='United States', Y='of America',Z iss X++' '++Y.

will cause an error. The **join2** predicate cannot deal with an argument such as **X++' '**.

As for factorial, we need to process the arguments on either side of ++ to ensure that they are strings (atoms), not expressions, before they are used. To do this we define a predicate **convert/2.** If the first argument is an atom, it binds the second argument to that value. If not, it must be an expression using ++, such as **'hello'++'world'**. In this case **iss** is used to calculate the new string and this is returned as the second argument.

The built-in predicate **atom/1** tests whether or not a term is an atom. The goal **atom(X)** succeeds if and only if **X** is an atom or a variable bound to an atom. Using this we can define the **convert/2** predicate as follows:

```
convert(X,X):-atom(X).
convert(X,X1):-X1 iss X.
```

The previous definition of ++ can now be replaced by the clause:

```
S iss S1++S2:-
    convert(S1,A),convert(S2,B),join2(A,B,S),!.
```

With this new definition, ++ can be used to join any number of strings together.

?- S iss 'hello'++' world'.
S = 'hello world'

?- X='United States', Y='of America',Z iss X++' '++Y.
X = 'United States' ,
Y = 'of America' ,

Z = 'United States of America'

?- X='United States', Y='of America',Z iss 'This is the '++X++' '++Y.
X = 'United States' ,
Y = 'of America' ,
Z = 'This is the United States of America'

11.4 Extending Prolog: Sets

An important branch of mathematics is known as *set theory*. A detailed description of this is outside the scope of this book, but essentially a set is similar to a list of atoms, such as [*a,b,c,d*] but with two major differences: the order of the elements is of no significance and no element may occur twice in a set.

Given two sets **X** and **Y,** a standard requirement is to produce any or all of three new sets based on the first two:

- the *intersection* – those elements that are in both sets
- the *union* – those elements that are in either set (or both)
- the *difference* – those elements that are in the first set but not the second.

We will denote these by the expressions **X and Y**, **X or Y** and **X−Y**, respectively.

To define these set operations, we will start by defining a new predicate **sis/2**, in the same way as **iss/2** was defined previously, i.e. by entering a goal such as

?- op(710,xfx,sis).

We now need to define the **and** and **or** operators for *intersection* and *union*, which we can do by entering goals such as:

?- op(200,yfx,and).
?-op(200,yfx,or).

There is no need to define the minus operator for *difference*, as it is already defined.

We now need to define the meaning of **and, or** and - when used in conjunction with **sis**. We do this using the predicate **findall/3**:

```
Y sis A and B :-
    findall(X,(member(X,A),member(X,B)),Y),!.
Y sis A or B :-
    findall(X,(member(X,A);member(X,B)),Y),!.
Y sis A−B :-
    findall(X,(member(X,A),not(member(X,B))),Y),!.
```

corresponding to find all elements that are members of both A and B, members of either A or B (or both) and members of A but not B, respectively. Unfortunately the second clause is not quite correct.

?- X=[a,b,c,d],Y=[e,b,f,c,g],A sis X and Y.
X = [a,b,c,d] ,
Y = [e,b,f,c,g] ,
A = [b,c]

?- X=[a,b,c,d],Y=[e,b,f,c,g],A sis X or Y.
X = [a,b,c,d],
Y = [e,b,f,c,g],
A = [a,b,c,d,e,b,f,c,g]

?- X=[a,b,c,d],Y=[e,b,f,c,g],A sis X−Y.
X = [a,b,c,d],
Y = [e,b,f,c,g],
A = [a,d]

The goal **A sis X or Y** causes variable **A** to be bound to a list containing all those elements that are in either **X** or **Y**. However elements *b* and *c* occur in both **X** and **Y**, and so appear twice in list **A**, which is therefore not a valid set.

To get around this, we can change the definition of the **or** operator to:

```
Y sis A or B:-
findall(X,(member(X,A);(member(X,B),
    not(member(X,A))))),Y),!.
```

corresponding to: find all elements *X* that are members of **A** or are members of **B** but not members of **A**.

With this new definition, the **or** operator gives the expected result.

?- X=[a,b,c,d],Y=[e,b,f,c,g],A sis X or Y.
X = [a,b,c,d],
Y = [e,b,f,c,g],
A = [a,b,c,d,e,f,g]

If we want to combine several operators in a single expression, e.g. **X and Y and Z**, we need to change the definitions of **and**, **or** and **-** when used with **sis**, to allow for the possibility of an argument being an expression not a list.

We can do this by first applying **sis** to each argument, replacing it by a list if it is an expression, or by itself if it is a list. This requires an additional final clause to be added, specifying that applying **sis** to 'anything else' (i.e. a list) gives the same value.

This gives a revised definition of **sis/2** as follows:

```
Y sis A and B :-
    A1 sis A,B1 sis B,
    findall(X,(member(X,A1),member(X,B1)),Y),!.

Y sis A or B:-
    A1 sis A,B1 sis B,
    findall(X,(member(X,A1);(member(X,B1),
    not(member(X,A1)))),Y),!.


Y sis A—B :-
    A1 sis A,B1 sis B,
    findall(X,(member(X,A1),not(member(X,B1))),Y),
    !.

A sis A:-!.
```

?- X=[a,b,c,d],Y=[e,b,f,c,g],Z=[a,e,c,g,h],A sis X and Y and Z.
X = [a,b,c,d] ,
Y = [e,b,f,c,g] ,
Z = [a,e,c,g,h] ,
A = [c]

?- X=[a,b,c,d],Y=[e,b,f,c,g],Z=[a,e,c,g,h],A sis X or Y or Z.
X = [a,b,c,d] ,
Y = [e,b,f,c,g] ,
Z = [a,e,c,g,h] ,
A = [a,b,c,d,e,f,g,h]

?- X=[a,b,c,d],Y=[e,b,f,c,g],Z=[a,e,c,g,h],A sis X−Y−Z.
X = [a,b,c,d] ,
Y = [e,b,f,c,g] ,
Z = [a,e,c,g,h] ,
A = [d]

11.5 Processing Terms

Prolog has several facilities for processing terms, which can be useful for more
advanced applications. Terms can be decomposed into their functor and arity, a
specified argument can be extracted from a compound term, terms can be converted
to lists or vice versa and a term can be evaluated as a goal.

Using the *univ* Operator to Convert Lists to Terms

The built-in infix operator =.. is known (for obscure historical reasons) as 'univ'. The operator is written as an = sign followed by two full stops, i.e. three characters.
Evaluating the goal

X=.. [member,A,L]

causes variable *X* to be bound to the term **member(A,L)**.
Evaluating the goal

X=..[colour,red]

causes *X* to be bound to the term **colour(red)**. *X* can then be used just like any other term, so for example

?-X=..[colour,red],assertz(X).

would place the clause **colour(red)** in the database.

?- X=..[colour,red],assertz(X).
X = colour(red)

?- colour(red).
true.

It is also possible to go the other way. If the first argument of 'univ' is a term and the second is an unbound variable, the latter is bound to a list that corresponds to the term, with the first element the functor and the remaining elements the arguments of the compound term in order. For example,

?- data(6,green,mypred(26,blue))=..L.

will bind the variable *L* to a list

L = [data,6,green,mypred(26,blue)]

The call/1 Predicate

The **call/1** predicate takes a single argument, which must be a call term, i.e. an atom or a compound term, or a variable bound to a call term. The term is evaluated as if it were a goal.

?- call(write('hello world')).
hello world
true.

?- X=write('hello world'),call(X).
hello world
X = write('hello world')

call/1 can be used to evaluate more than one goal if they are separated by commas and enclosed in parentheses.

?- call((write('hello world'),nl,write('goodbye world'),nl)).
hello world
goodbye world
true.

?- X=(write('hello world'),nl),call(X).
hello world
X = (write('hello world'),nl)

In the above cases there is no benefit over entering the goal or goals directly. However, if the value of X is not known in advance but is a calculated value or is read from a file, being able to call X as a goal can be very useful.

The **call** predicate is sometimes used in conjunction with *univ*, for example:

?- X=..[write,'hello world'],call(X).
hello world
X = write('hello world')

If the database contains the clause

```
greet(Z):-write('Hello '),write(Z),nl,
write('How are you?'),nl.
```

we can cause a **greet** goal to be evaluated by:

?- X=..[greet,martin],call(X).
Hello martin
How are you?
X = greet(martin)

The functor/3 Predicate

The built-in predicate **functor/3** takes three arguments. If the first argument is an atom or a compound term or a variable bound to one of those, and the other two arguments are unbound, the second argument will be bound to the functor of the first argument and the third will be bound to its arity. For this purpose an atom is considered to have arity zero.

?- functor(write('hello world'),A,B).
A = write ,
B = 1

?- functor(city(london,england,europe),Funct,Ar).
Funct = city ,
Ar = 3

?- Z=person(a,b,c,d),functor(Z,F,A).
Z = person(a,b,c,d) ,
F = person ,
A = 4

?- functor(start,F,A).
F = start ,
A = 0

?- functor(a+b,F,A).
F = (+) ,
A = 2

If the first argument is an unbound variable, the second is an atom, and the third is a positive integer, the variable is bound to a compound term with the given functor and arity, with all its arguments unbound variables. If the third argument is zero, the first argument is bound to an atom.

?- functor(T,person,4).
T = person(_42952,_42954,_42956,_42958)

?- functor(T,start,0).
T = start

The arg/3 Predicate

The built-in predicate **arg/3** can be used to find a specified argument of a compound term. The first two arguments must be bound to a positive integer and a compound term, respectively. If the third argument is an unbound variable, it is bound to the value of the specified argument of the compound term.

?- arg(3,person(mary,jones,doctor,london),X).
X = doctor

?- N=2,T=person(mary,jones,doctor,london),arg(N,T,X).
N = 2 ,
T = person(mary,jones,doctor,london) ,
X = jones

We can use **functor/3** and **arg/3** to define a predicate to determine whether or not two call terms will unify, as described in Section 3.2. The built-in operator =/2 can be used for this, but we shall assume that it is not available. In summary, an atom can only be unified with the same atom and a compound term can only be unified with a compound term with the same functor and arity. Two compound terms with the same functor and arity unify if and only if their arguments unify pairwise. A first version of a **unify/2** predicate embodying these rules is as follows.

```
unify(CT1,CT2):-
    functor(CT1,Funct1,Arity1),
    functor(CT2,Funct2,Arity2),
    compare(Funct1,Arity1,Funct2,Arity2).
compare(F,0,F,0). /* Same atom*/
compare(F,0,F1,0):-fail.
/* Will not unify - different atoms */
compare(F,A,F,A):-write('May unify - check whether
arguments unify pairwise'),nl.
compare(_,_,_,_):-fail.
```

?- **unify(person(a,b,c,d),person(a,b,c))**.
false.

?- **unify(person(a,b,c,d),person2(a,b,c,d))**.
false.

?- **unify(london,london)**.
true.

?- **unify(london,washington)**.
false.

?- **unify(dog,person(a,b))**.
false.

?- **unify(person(a,b,c,d),person(a,b,c,f))**.
May unify - check whether arguments unify pairwise
true.

To extend this program we need to modify the penultimate **compare** clause. We start by adding two additional arguments to predicate **compare,** so we can pass the two call terms to it from **unify.** We then change the penultimate clause of **compare** so that when the call terms are both compound terms with the same functor and arity they are passed to a new predicate **unify2,** which examines their arguments pairwise.

unify2 works by converting the two compound terms to lists using *univ,* then removing the heads of the lists (the common functor) and passing them to predicate **paircheck/2,** which succeeds if and only if the corresponding pairs of list elements can be unified. The standard Prolog unification is used to check that each pair of elements can be unified.

```
unify(CT1,CT2):-
    functor(CT1,Funct1,Arity1),
    functor(CT2,Funct2,Arity2),
    compare(CT1,CT2,Funct1,Arity1,Funct2,Arity2).
compare(CT1,CT2,F,0,F,0). /* Same atom*/
compare(CT1,CT2,F,0,F1,0):-fail. /* Different atoms */
compare(CT1,CT2,F,A,F,A):-unify2(CT1,CT2),!.
compare(CT1,CT2,_,_,_,_):-fail.
unify2(CT1,CT2):-
    CT1=..[F|L1],CT2=..[F|L2],!,paircheck(L1,L2).
paircheck([],[]).
paircheck([A|L1],[A|L2]):-paircheck(L1,L2).
```

?- **unify(person(a,b,c,d),person(a,b,c,f)).**
false.

?- **unify(person(a,b,c,d),person(a,b,X,Y)).**
X = c ,
Y= d

?- **unify(pred(6,A,[X,Y,[a,b,c]],pred2(p,q)),pred(P1,Q1,L,Z)).**
A = Q1 ,
P1 = 6 ,
L = [X,Y,[a,b,c]] ,
Z = pred2(p,q)

?- **unify(person(a,b,c,d),person(a,b,X,X)).**
false.

Note that this definition of **unify** is a simplified one that does not ensure that there are no common variables in the two compound terms. This needs to be dealt with separately.

Chapter Summary

This chapter describes some of the more advanced features provided by Prolog: the use of operators to extend the language (e.g. to provide new arithmetic operators, improved facilities for processing strings or facilities for processing sets) and facilities for processing terms, including finding their functors and arities, extracting a specified argument of a term, converting terms to lists or evaluating terms as goals. A user-defined predicate to unify two compound terms is given.

Practical Exercise 11

(1) Extend the definition of the **iss/2** predicate with prefix operators for the head and tail of a list that can be used in the following way:

?- Y iss head [a,b,c].
Y = a

?- Y iss tail [a,b,c].
Y = [b,c]

(2) Define and test a predicate **addArg/3.** Its first argument must be a compound term or a variable bound to one. The second argument must be a term. The third argument must be an unbound variable. Evaluating the goal should bind this variable to a compound term that is the same as the original one, with the specified term added as an additional final argument. Your definition should work however many arguments the compound term used for the first argument has. For example, it should produce the following output:

?- addArg(person(john,smith,25),london,T).
T = person(john,smith,25,london)

Chapter 12
Using Grammar Rules to Analyse English Sentences

Chapter Aims

After reading this chapter you should be able to:

- Understand and use the special syntax provided in Prolog for analyzing grammar rules.
- Define a simple grammar able to deal with basic sentences of English.
- Define predicates to enable the validity of sentences presented as lists of words to be established and to extract important information such as the type of each noun phrase from valid sentences.
- Define predicates to convert sentences in standard English into the 'list of words' form required by Prolog grammar rules.

12.1 Introduction

In this and the next chapter we will end the book by illustrating some of the uses to which Prolog can be put. We will focus on applications from the world of Artificial Intelligence (AI) as that was the field in which Prolog was originally developed.

As this is not a textbook on AI, the examples chosen may seem quite rudimentary, but do not be fooled by this. Prolog is a powerful language for AI projects in which some very substantial systems have been written.

12.2 Parsing English Sentences

Processing natural language (particularly sentences in English) was one of the earliest application areas for Prolog and no doubt largely because of this there is a special syntax available to support it in most versions of the language.

M. Bramer, *Logic Programming with Prolog*, DOI 10.1007/978-1-4471-5487-7_12,
© Springer-Verlag London 2013

We start by looking at how Prolog can be used to break down sentences of English into their component parts (nouns, verbs etc.), which is known as *parsing*. Do not worry – this is not going to turn into a book on the grammar of English so all the sentences we use for illustration will be very basic ones.

We can think of a simple English sentence having the form 'a noun, followed by a verb, followed by a noun', or even simpler: 'a noun followed by a verb'. In Prolog we can define a sentence this way by the two clauses:

```
sentence-->noun,verb,noun.
sentence-->noun,verb.
```

The –>*/2* operator can be read as 'is a' or 'comprises' or 'is made up of'. So the first clause indicates that a sentence can comprise a noun, followed by a verb, followed by a noun. As usual in Prolog we place the more specific clause before the more general one. (Note that the –> operator is three keystrokes: two hyphens followed by a 'greater than' symbol.)

This would be a possible way of defining sentences, but is very limited. It would allow 'man saw' and 'man saw dog' but not 'the man saw a dog'. Our first improvement to the above prototype program will be to change *noun* to '*noun_phrase*' which we will define as an optional determiner followed by a noun. (The words 'the', 'a' and 'an' are called *determiners*.)

This change brings us closer to a usable definition of a sentence, but we also need to define some nouns and verbs. Putting all these definitions together gives us a first version of a Prolog program defining the grammar of a very restricted version of English.

```
sentence-->noun_phrase,verb,noun_phrase.
sentence-->noun_phrase,verb.

noun_phrase-->determiner,noun.
noun_phrase-->noun.

verb-->[sat].
verb-->[saw].
verb-->[hears].
verb-->[took].
verb-->[sees].

determiner-->[the].
determiner-->[a].
determiner-->[an].
```

```
noun-->[cat].
noun-->[mat].
noun-->[man].
noun-->[boy].
noun-->[dog].
```

Terms such as *sentence*, *noun_phrase* and *verb* are called *syntactic terms*, to indicate that they are part of the structure of the English language. The list brackets around [mat] etc. are used to indicate that they are actual words in the language, not syntactic terms. Such words are often called *terminals*. Terminals can also be characters such as ',' or '?'.

The usual rules for Prolog atoms apply to syntactic terms such as *sentence* and *noun_phrase* and terminals such as *sat* and *took*, i.e. if they comprise only lower case letters, underscores and digits starting with a lower case letter they can be written without surrounding quotes, but any that begin with a capital letter, a digit or a symbol such as a question mark must be enclosed in quotes. This is why we wrote '?' above. In practice it is easiest to keep to lower case words.

We can now check whether a sentence such as 'the cat saw the mat' is valid in our restricted language. Prolog provides a special predicate **phrase/2** to do this. It takes two arguments: the first is a syntactic term such as *sentence* or *noun_phrase* (the left hand side of one of the –> operators) and the second is a list of words. So to check whether 'the cat saw the mat' is a valid sentence we can simply enter the query:

?- phrase(sentence,[the,cat,saw,the,mat]).
true .

The sequence of words 'the cat mat' is not a valid sentence, however.

?- phrase(sentence,[the,cat,mat]).
false.

A grammar such as the one above is called a 'definite clause grammar'. It is a 'context free' grammar, in the sense that it takes no account of the meaning of words, just whether they match the structure of the language (its syntax). Thus 'the mat saw the cat' is also a valid sentence.

?- phrase(sentence,[the,mat,saw,the,cat]).
true .

We can also test whether a sequence of words is a valid form of another syntactic term, such as a *noun_phrase*, e.g.

?- phrase(noun_phrase,[a,cat]).
true .

As this is Prolog we can also enter more complex queries, such as which words can validly come at the end of a sentence beginning 'the cat saw the':

?- phrase(sentence,[the,cat,saw,the,X]).
X = cat;
X = mat;
X = man;
X = boy;
X = dog;
false.

or which single word can end a sentence starting 'the cat saw'.

?- phrase(sentence,[the,cat,saw,X]).
X = cat;
X = mat;
X = man;
X = boy;
X = dog;
false.

or which two words can end a sentence beginning 'the cat saw':

?- phrase(sentence,[the,cat,saw,X,Y]).
X = the,
Y = cat;
X = the,
Y = mat;
X = the,
Y = man;
[etc.]

We can represent a compound verb such as 'will see' by a single word with an embedded underscore.

```
verb-->[will_see].
```

?- phrase(sentence,[the,man,will_see,the,cat]).
true .

We can now elaborate our language by introducing adjectives between the determiner and the noun in a *noun_phrase*, e.g. a large brown cat.

To allow for one adjective we can add an extra clause to the definition of *noun_phrase* giving

```
noun_phrase-->determiner,adjective,noun.
noun_phrase-->determiner,noun.
noun_phrase-->noun.
```

and define some adjectives, e.g.

```
adjective-->[large].
adjective-->[small].
adjective-->[brown].
adjective-->[orange].
adjective-->[green].
adjective-->[blue].
```

With this improved grammar we can verify some more complex sentences, e.g.:

?- phrase(sentence,[the,blue,cat,saw,the,large,man]).
true .

If we want to allow for a sequence of adjectives rather than just one, we can define an *adjective_sequence* which is either an adjective or an adjective followed by an *adjective_sequence*.

To do this change the first line in the definition of *noun_phrase* to

```
noun_phrase-->determiner,adjective_sequence,noun.
```

and add the definition of adjective_sequence

```
adjective_sequence-->adjective,adjective_sequence.
adjective_sequence-->adjective.
```

We can then verify quite lengthy sentences such as

?-   phrase(sentence,[the,large,orange,man,saw,the,small,brown,orange,green, dog]).
true .

Before going any further, we need to step back and consider the clauses shown in this section so far. Although they certainly have a resemblance to them, they are not Prolog clauses (rules and facts) as defined and used elsewhere in this book. Clauses using the –> operator may be mixed freely with 'regular' Prolog clauses in a Prolog program and are essentially regular clauses 'in disguise'. For example the clause

```
verb-->[took].
```

is a 'disguised' form of the 'regular' Prolog clause (fact)

```
verb([took|A], A).
```

The latest version of the program developed in this section is as follows:

```
sentence-->noun_phrase,verb,noun_phrase.
sentence-->noun_phrase,verb.

noun_phrase-->determiner,adjective_sequence,noun.
noun_phrase-->determiner,noun.
noun_phrase-->noun.

verb-->[sat].
verb-->[saw].
verb-->[hears].
verb-->[took].
verb-->[sees].
verb-->[will_see].

adjective_sequence-->adjective,adjective_sequence.
adjective_sequence-->adjective.

determiner-->[the].
determiner-->[a].
determiner-->[an].

noun-->[cat].
noun-->[mat].
noun-->[man].
noun-->[boy].
noun-->[dog].

adjective-->[large].
adjective-->[small].
adjective-->[brown].
adjective-->[orange].
adjective-->[green].
adjective-->[blue].
```

If we use **the listing/1** predicate to see which rules and facts are in the database for predicates *sentence*, *noun_phrase*, *verb* etc. in turn, we can see that the above program is in fact stored as the 'regular' Prolog clauses:

```
sentence(A, D) :-
        noun_phrase(A, B),
        verb(B, C),
        noun_phrase(C, D).
sentence(A, C) :-
        noun_phrase(A, B),
        verb(B, C).

noun_phrase(A, D) :-
        determiner(A, B),
        adjective_sequence(B, C),
        noun(C, D).
noun_phrase(A, C) :-
        determiner(A, B),
        noun(B, C).
noun_phrase(A, B) :-
        noun(A, B).

verb([sat|A], A).
verb([saw|A], A).
verb([hears|A], A).
verb([took|A], A).
verb([sees|A], A).
verb([will_see|A], A).

adjective_sequence(A, C) :-
        adjective(A, B),
        adjective_sequence(B, C).
adjective_sequence(A, B) :-
        adjective(A, B).

determiner([the|A], A).
determiner([a|A], A).
determiner([an|A], A).

noun([cat|A], A).
noun([mat|A], A).
```

```
noun([man|A], A).
noun([boy|A], A).
noun([dog|A], A).

adjective([large|A], A).
adjective([small|A], A).
adjective([brown|A], A).
adjective([orange|A], A).
adjective([green|A], A).
adjective([blue|A], A).
```

This is considerably different! For example the syntactic term *sentence* has become the predicate **sentence** with two arguments. This is what was meant by saying that a special syntax is available for language parsing in Section 12.2. The $->$ operator is not merely an infix operator, using it enables a different syntax for Prolog to be used that is automatically converted to 'regular' Prolog clauses.

Special language syntax of this form is sometimes known by the slightly derogatory term *syntactic sugar*. The implication is presumably that 'real' programmers do not need such sweetening on top of their favourite language. While this may be true, there is no doubt that most people will find it much easier to work with Prolog clauses for language processing written using the $->$ notation than with the 'raw' Prolog clauses generated from them.

We will next show how the grammar rule notation can be used to ensure that a singular noun is followed by a singular verb and a plural noun is followed by a plural verb, i.e. that a noun and the following verb have the same *plurality*.

We first change the definition of our five nouns to

```
noun(singular)-->[cat].
noun(singular)-->[mat].
noun(singular)-->[man].
noun(singular)-->[boy].
noun(singular)-->[dog].
```

and then add the plural forms

```
noun(plural)-->[cats].
noun(plural)-->[mats].
noun(plural)-->[men].
noun(plural)-->[boys].
noun(plural)-->[dogs].
```

We next do the same for the verbs

```
verb(both)-->[sat].
verb(both)-->[saw].
verb(both)-->[took].
verb(both)-->[will_see].

verb(singular)-->[hears].
verb(singular)-->[sees].

verb(plural)-->[hear].
verb(plural)-->[see].
```

The first four verbs are labelled 'both', indicating that they are the same with either a singular or a plural noun ('the man sat', 'the men sat' etc.). Verbs 'hears' and 'sees' are labelled as 'singular' and we have added the plural forms 'hear' and 'see'.

We can now change the definitions of *sentence* and *noun_phrase* to incorporate information about the plurality of the first noun and the corresponding verb.

```
sentence-->noun_phrase(_),verb(both),noun_phrase(_).
sentence-->noun_phrase(_),verb(both).

sentence-->noun_phrase(Plurality),verb(Plurality),
    noun_phrase(_).
sentence-->noun_phrase(Plurality),verb(Plurality).

noun_phrase(Plurality)-->determiner,
    adjective_sequence,noun(Plurality).
noun_phrase(Plurality)-->determiner,noun(Plurality).
noun_phrase(Plurality)-->noun(Plurality).
```

The definition of *sentence* indicates that if the plurality of the verb is 'both' we do not care about the plurality of the preceding noun. However if the verb has a plurality that is 'singular' or 'plural' we require the first noun in the sentence to have the same plurality as the verb. In all cases we are unconcerned about the plurality of the second noun (if there is one).

?- **phrase(sentence,[the,small,green,man,sees,a,large,dog]).**
true.

?- **phrase(sentence,[the,small,green,men,sees,a,large,dog]).**
false.

?- **phrase(sentence,[the,small,green,men,see,a,large,dog]).**
true.

?- phrase(sentence,[the,small,green,man,sees,the,large,dogs]).
true .

?- phrase(sentence,[the,small,green,man,took,the,large,dogs]).
true .

?- phrase(sentence,[the,small,green,men,took,the,large,dogs]).
true .

It would be straightforward to associate a tense (past, present or future) with a verb in the same way that we have associated a plurality with nouns and verbs, but we will not pursue this possibility here.

Instead we will demonstrate that it is possible to include 'regular' Prolog in a grammar rule clause. To do this we make use of another piece of special syntax and enclose the 'regular' Prolog in {braces}.

Instead of the six grammar rules currently defining adjectives we can write:

```
adjective-->[X],{adjective_is(X)}.

adjective_is(large).
adjective_is(small).

adjective-->[brown].
adjective-->[orange].
adjective-->[green].
adjective-->[blue].
```

The first clause indicates that an *adjective* is any X such that *adjective_is(X)*. The other definitions of *adjective* (green etc.) could also have been converted into *adjective_is* form, of course, but they have been left as they were to indicate that a mixed notation is possible.

?- phrase(sentence,[the,man,saw,the,large,dog]).
true .

?- phrase(sentence,[the,man,saw,the,large,green,dog]).
true .

?- phrase(sentence,[the,green,man,saw,the,small,blue,large,boy]).
true .

Now we have the {brace} notation available, we can simplify the whole definition of *adjective* to the much more compact form:

```
adjective-->[X],
    {member(X,[large,small,brown,orange,green,blue])}.
```

?- phrase(sentence,[the,small,green,man,saw,the,large,orange,green,dog]).
true .

We can also simplify the definition of singular and plural nouns to just:

```
noun(singular)-->[X],{member(X,[cat,mat,man,
   boy,dog])}.
noun(plural)-->[X],{member(X,[cats,mats,men,
   boys,dogs])}.
```

?- phrase(sentence,[the,small,green,man,sees,a,large,dog]).
true .

?- phrase(sentence,[the,small,green,men,sees,a,large,dog]).
false.

?- phrase(sentence,[the,small,green,men,see,a,large,dog]).
true .

?- phrase(sentence,[the,small,green,man,sees,the,large,dogs]).
true .

?- phrase(sentence,[the,small,green,man,took,the,large,dogs]).
true .

?- phrase(sentence,[the,small,green,men,took,the,large,dogs]).
true .

Similarly the definition of *verb* can be simplified to:

```
verb(both)-->[X],{member(X,[sat,saw,took,will_see])}.
verb(singular)-->[X],{member(X,[hears,sees])}.
verb(plural)-->[X],{member(X,[hear,see])}.
```

As well as wishing to verify that a sentence is syntactically valid we may wish to show which of the four types of valid sentence we have defined applies in a particular case. We can do this by adding an argument to each of the *sentence* clauses.

```
sentence(s1)-->noun_phrase(_),verb(both),
   noun_phrase(_).
sentence(s2)-->noun_phrase(Plurality),verb(Plurality),
   noun_phrase(_).
sentence(s3)-->noun_phrase(_),verb(both).
sentence(s4)-->noun_phrase(Plurality),verb(Plurality).
```

?- phrase(sentence(Stype),[the,blue,man,saw,a,large,green,boy]).
Stype = s1 .

?- phrase(sentence(Stype),[the,small,green,men,hear]).
Stype = s4 .

We may also want to know which of the definitions of *noun_phrase* have been used. We can give them labels too:

```
noun_phrase(np1,Plurality)-->determiner,
    adjective_sequence,noun(Plurality).
noun_phrase(np2,Plurality)-->determiner,
    noun(Plurality).
noun_phrase(np3,Plurality)-->noun(Plurality).
```

There may be either one or two *noun_phrases* in a valid sentence. To allow for this, we could define two versions of *sentence*, one with two arguments (the *sentence* type, followed by the single *noun_phrase* type) and the other with three arguments (the *sentence* type and then two *noun_phrase* types).

However it is probably preferable for *sentence* to have a single argument which is a list. The first element of the list is always the *sentence* type (s1, s2 etc.). The rest of the list comprises the type of the one or two *noun_phrases* (np1,np2 etc.) that appear in the sentence, as appropriate.

```
sentence([s1,NP1,NP2])-->noun_phrase(NP1,_),
    verb(both),noun_phrase(NP2,_).
sentence([s2,NP1,NP2])-->noun_phrase(NP1,Plurality),
    verb(Plurality),noun_phrase(NP2,_).
sentence([s3,NP1])-->noun_phrase(NP1,_),verb(both).
sentence([s4,NP1])-->noun_phrase(NP1,Plurality),
    verb(Plurality).
```

?-phrase(sentence(S),[the,large,green,men,see,a,small,blue,dog]).
S = [s2, np1, np1] .

There is a valid sentence of type s2, with two noun_phrases, both of type np1.

?- phrase(sentence(S),[the,men,saw,dogs]).
S = [s1, np2, np3] .

?- phrase(sentence(S),[the,green,men,took]).
S = [s3, np1] .

We can also include the plurality of the verb as the second element of the list by changing the definition of *sentence* as follows:

```
sentence([s1,both,NP1,NP2])-->noun_phrase(NP1,_),
    verb(both),noun_phrase(NP2,_).
sentence([s2,Plurality,NP1,NP2])-->noun_phrase
    (NP1,Plurality),verb(Plurality),noun_phrase(NP2,_).
sentence([s3,both,NP1])-->noun_phrase(NP1,_)
    ,verb(both).
sentence([s4,Plurality,NP1])-->noun_phrase
    (NP1,Plurality),verb(Plurality).
```

?- phrase(sentence(S),[the,large,green,men,see,a,small,blue,dog]).
S = [s2, plural, np1, np1] .

?- phrase(sentence(S),[the,men,saw,dogs]).
S = [s1, both, np2, np3] .

?- phrase(sentence(S),[the,green,men,took]).
S = [s3, both, np1] .

This is clearly moving away from merely verifying that a sentence is syntactically valid to something closer to a linguistic analysis of the structure of the sentence.

We can add the verb itself as the third element of the list by changing the definitions of *sentence* and *verb*.

```
sentence([s1,both,V,NP1,NP2])-->noun_phrase(NP1,_),
    verb(both,V),noun_phrase(NP2,_).
sentence([s2,Plurality,V,NP1,NP2])
-->noun_phrase(NP1,Plurality),
    verb(Plurality,V),noun_phrase(NP2,_).
sentence([s3,both,V,NP1])-->noun_phrase(NP1,_),
verb(both,V).
sentence([s4,Plurality,V,NP1])
-->noun_phrase(NP1,Plurality),verb(Plurality,V).

verb(both,X)-->[X],{member(X,[sat,saw,
    took,will_see])}.
verb(singular,X)-->[X],{member(X,[hears,sees])}.
verb(plural,X)-->[X],{member(X,[hear,see])}.
```

?- phrase(sentence(S),[the,large,green,men,see,a,small,blue,dog]).
S = [s2, plural, see, np1, np1] .

?- phrase(sentence(S),[the,large,green,men,will_see,a,small,blue,dog]).
S = [s1, both, will_see, np1, np1] .

?- phrase(sentence(S),[the,green,small,men,see,a,blue,dog]).

S = [s2, plural, see, np1, np1] .

?- phrase(sentence(S),[the,green,small,men,took,a,blue,dog]).
S = [s1, both, took, np1, np1] .

?- phrase(sentence(S),[the,green,small,man,sees]).
S = [s4, singular, sees, np1] .

If we also want to get the noun or nouns into the list we can do so, starting by changing the definition of a *noun* to include as the second argument the word itself. Then we change the definition of *noun_phrase* to have a third argument, the noun word itself. Finally, we change the definition of *sentence* to put the noun or nouns into the list that is the argument of *sentence*.

```
sentence([s1,both,V,NP1,Noun1,NP2,Noun2])
-->noun_phrase(NP1,_,Noun1),
    verb(both,V),noun_phrase(NP2,_,Noun2).
sentence([s2,Plurality,V,NP1,Noun1,NP2,Noun2]
-->noun_phrase(NP1,Plurality,Noun1),
    verb(Plurality,V),noun_phrase(NP2,_,Noun2).
sentence([s3,both,V,NP1,Noun1])
-->noun_phrase(NP1,_,Noun1),verb(both,V).
sentence([s4,Plurality,V,NP1,Noun1])
-->noun_phrase(NP1,Plurality,Noun1),
    verb(Plurality,V).

noun_phrase(np1,Plurality,N)-->determiner,
    adjective_sequence,noun(Plurality,N).
```

```
noun_phrase(np2,Plurality,N)-->determiner,
    noun(Plurality,N).
noun_phrase(np3,Plurality,N)-->noun(Plurality,N).

noun(singular,X)-->[X],{member(X,[cat,mat,man,
    boy,dog])}.
noun(plural,X)-->[X],{member(X,[cats,mats,men,
    boys,dogs])}.
```

?- phrase(sentence(S),[the,green,small,men,see,a,blue,dog]).
S = [s2, plural, see, np1, men, np1, dog] .

?- phrase(sentence(S),[the,green,small,men,took,a,blue,dog]).
S = [s1, both, took, np1, men, np1, dog] .

?- phrase(sentence(S),[the,green,small,man,sees]).
S = [s4, singular, sees, np1, man] .

?- phrase(sentence(S),[the,green,small,men,will_see,a,blue,dog]).
S = [s1, both, will_see, np1, men, np1, dog] .

Finally, we may wish to compile a list of all the verbs that occur in a sequence of valid sentences that we analyse. This can be done by adding an **assertz** goal at the end of each of the four definitions of *sentence*.

```
sentence([s1,both,V,NP1,Noun1,NP2,Noun2])
-->noun_phrase(NP1,_,Noun1),verb(both,V),
    noun_phrase(NP2,_,Noun2),{assertz(wordlist
    (verb,both,V))}.
sentence([s2,Plurality,V,NP1,Noun1,NP2,Noun2])
-->noun_phrase(NP1,Plurality,Noun1),
    verb(Plurality,V),noun_phrase(NP2,_,Noun2),
    {assertz(wordlist(verb,Plurality,V))}.
sentence([s3,both,V,NP1,Noun1])-->noun_phrase
    (NP1,_,Noun1),
    verb(both,V),{assertz(wordlist(verb,both,V))}.
sentence([s4,Plurality,V,NP1,Noun1])
-->noun_phrase(NP1,Plurality,Noun1),
    verb(Plurality,V),{assertz(wordlist
    (verb,Plurality,V))}.
```

?- phrase(sentence(S),[the,man,sees,the,blue,green,small,dog]).
S = [s2, singular, sees, np2, man, np1, dog] .

?- phrase(sentence(S),[the,man,took,the,blue,green,small,dog]).
S = [s1, both, took, np2, man, np1, dog] .

?- phrase(sentence(S),[a,large,man,sees,the,blue,green,small,dog]).
S = [s2, singular, sees, np1, man, np1, dog] .

?- phrase(sentence(S),[the,men,hear,the,blue,green,small,dog]).
S = [s2, plural, hear, np2, men, np1, dog] .

?- listing(wordlist).

wordlist(verb, singular, sees).
wordlist(verb, both, took).
wordlist(verb, singular, sees).
wordlist(verb, plural, hear).

true.

There is clearly much more that could be done, but we will leave the parsing of English here. For reference, the complete program developed in this section is given below.

```
sentence([s1,both,V,NP1,Noun1,NP2,Noun2])
-->noun_phrase(NP1,_,Noun1),verb(both,V),
   noun_phrase(NP2,_,Noun2),{assertz(wordlist
   (verb,both,V))}.
sentence([s2,Plurality,V,NP1,Noun1,NP2,Noun2])
-->noun_phrase(NP1,Plurality,Noun1),verb(Plurality,V),
   noun_phrase(NP2,_,Noun2),
   {assertz(wordlist(verb,Plurality,V))}.
sentence([s3,both,V,NP1,Noun1])-->noun_phrase
   (NP1,_,Noun1),
   verb(both,V),{assertz(wordlist(verb,both,V))}.
sentence([s4,Plurality,V,NP1,Noun1])
-->noun_phrase(NP1,Plurality,Noun1),
   verb(Plurality,V),{assertz(wordlist
   (verb,Plurality,V))}.

noun_phrase(np1,Plurality,N)-->determiner,
   adjective_sequence,noun(Plurality,N).
noun_phrase(np2,Plurality,N)-->determiner,noun
   (Plurality,N).
noun_phrase(np3,Plurality,N)-->noun(Plurality,N).

verb(both,X)-->[X],{member(X,[sat,saw,took,
   will_see])}.
verb(singular,X)-->[X],{member(X,[hears,sees])}.
verb(plural,X)-->[X],{member(X,[hear,see])}.

adjective_sequence-->adjective,adjective_sequence.
adjective_sequence-->adjective.

determiner-->[the].
determiner-->[a].
determiner-->[an].

noun(singular,X)-->[X],{member(X,[cat,mat,man,boy,
   dog])}.
noun(plural,X)-->[X],{member(X,[cats,mats,men,boys,
   dogs])}.

adjective-->[X],
   {member(X,[large,small,brown,orange,green,blue])}.
```

12.3 Converting Sentences to List Form

The most obvious difficulty with the use of grammar rule syntax and the **phrase/2** predicate is that sentences do not naturally come in neat lists of words. Rather they can be lengthy sequences of words, with embedded spaces, commas, colons etc.

To illustrate the issues involved in converting real sentences to lists of words we will make use of a file named *dickens.txt* which contains the first six sentences of the celebrated story 'A Christmas Carol' by Charles Dickens.

Marley was dead: to begin with.

There is no doubt whatever about that.
The register of his burial was signed by the clergyman, the clerk, the undertaker, and the chief mourner. Scrooge signed it. And Scrooge's name was good upon 'Change, for anything he chose to put his hand to.

Old Marley was as dead as a door-nail.

There are a number of points to note:

- A sentence can run over more than one line of the file.
- More than one sentence can appear on the same line.
- Sentences are separated by at least one space or end of line character.
- The final sentence is followed by a blank line and then an end-of-file marker.
- The words in sentences are separated by spaces, end of line characters or punctuation marks such as commas and colons.
- Sentences end with a terminator (full stop, exclamation mark or question mark, although only full stops are used in this example).
- Spaces, end of line characters, punctuation marks (such as commas and colons) and terminators (full stops, exclamation marks and question marks) should all be removed. However apostrophes are part of words such as Scrooge's and should not be removed.

Converting sentences to list form is difficult to do, much more so than most of the other programs in this book. A Prolog program to convert the *dickens.txt* file to six sentences in list form is given below without explanation but for possible use in the reader's own programs. As in Chapter 5 we will assume that the ASCII characters corresponding to 'end of line' and 'end of file' have ASCII values 10 and -1 respectively.

```
readlineF(File):-
see(File),repeat,inputline(L),L=[end_of_file],!,seen.

inputline(L):-buildlist(L,[]),reverse(L,L1),
    writeout(L1),!.

writeout([]).
writeout([end_of_file]).
writeout(L):-write('Sentence: '),write(L),nl.

buildlist(L,OldL):-findword(Word,[]),
(
    (Word=[],L=OldL);
    (Word=[end_of_file],L=[end_of_file]);
    (Word=[sep],buildlist(L,OldL));
    (Word=[termin|Word1],name(S,Word1),L=[S|OldL]);
    (name(S,Word),buildlist(L,[S|OldL]))
).

findword(Word,OldWord):-get0(X),
(
    (terminator(X),Word=[termin|OldWord]);
    (separator(X),((OldWord=[],Word=[sep]);
    Word=OldWord));
    (X<0,Word=[end_of_file]);
    (append(OldWord,[X],New),findword(Word,New))
).

separator(10). /* end of line */
separator(32). /* space*/
separator(44). /* comma */
separator(58). /* colon */

terminator(46). /* full stop */
terminator(33). /* exclamation mark */
terminator(63). /* question mark */
```

?- readlineF('dickens.txt').
Sentence: [Marley,was,dead,to,begin,with]
Sentence: [There,is,no,doubt,whatever,about,that]
Sentence: [The,register,of,his,burial,was,signed,by,the,clergyman,the,clerk,the,
undertaker,and,the,chief,mourner]
Sentence: [Scrooge,signed,it]

Sentence: [And,Scrooge's,name,was,good,upon,'Change,for,anything,he,chose, to,put,his,hand,to]
Sentence: [Old,Marley,was,as,dead,as,a,door-nail]
true.

One improvement to this program would be to replace all the words by their lower case equivalents, i.e. change 'There' to 'here', 'And' to 'and' etc. Words appearing at the start of a sentence are generally spelt with an initial capital letter and those that do not are generally spelt with an initial lower case letter. For a practical system for analyzing sentences standardizing all words to begin with a lower case letter (e.g. standardizing both 'There' and 'there' to 'there') reduces the number of words that have to be stored considerably. It can be achieved quite easily by adjusting the **get0(X)** goal in the first line of the definition of **findword** so that if the character input is an upper case letter (values 65 to 90 inclusive) it is changed to its lower case equivalent (97 to 122 inclusive). Other characters are left unchanged.

The first line of the definition of **findword** should be changed to:

```
findword(Word,OldWord):-get0(X1),repchar(X1,X),
```

A new predicate **repchar** also needs to be added, defined as follows.

```
repchar(X,New):-X>=65,X=<90,New is X+32,!.
repchar(Char,Char).
```

Now the effect of using readlineF is:

?- readlineF('dickens.txt').
Sentence: [marley,was,dead,to,begin,with]
Sentence: [there,is,no,doubt,whatever,about,that]
Sentence: [the,register,of,his,burial,was,signed,by,the,clergyman,the,clerk,the, undertaker,and,the,chief,mourner]
Sentence: [scrooge,signed,it]
Sentence: [and,scrooge's,name,was,good,upon,'change,for,anything,he,chose,to, put,his,hand,to]
Sentence: [old,marley,was,as,dead,as,a,door-nail]
true.

A second desirable change is to write the new sentences into a text file so that they can be read in again for subsequent processing. This can be achieved by giving the **readlineF** predicate an extra argument and changing its definition to

```
readlineF(File,Outfile):-
    see(File),tell(Outfile),repeat,inputline(L),
    L=[end_of_file],!,told,seen.
```

and changing the final clause of **writeout** to:

```
writeout(L):-writeq(L),write('.'),nl.
```

Note the use of the **writeq** rather than the **write** predicate here and also that each list is output with a full stop and a newline character after it.

?- readlineF('dickens.txt','newdickens.txt').
true.

The file *newdickens.txt* now contains

[marley,was,dead,to,begin,with].
[there,is,no,doubt,whatever,about,that].
[the,register,of,his,burial,was,signed,by,the,clergyman,the,clerk,the,
undertaker,and,the,chief,mourner].
[scrooge,signed,it].
[and,'scrooge \ 's',name,was,good,upon,' \ 'change',for,anything,he,
chose,to,put,his,hand,to].
[old,marley,was,as,dead,as,a,'door-nail'].

Thanks to the use of **writeq**, the original word Scrooge's has been changed to the atom 'scrooge\'s' enclosed in quotes and with the embedded quote character written as \'. Similarly Dickens's word 'Change (an archaic way of writing the word Exchange) has been changed to '\'change'.

In this form each list is a valid Prolog term, terminated by a full stop, which can be processed by a separate Prolog program which analyses the contents of sentences.

The extract from 'A Christmas Carol' was chosen to illustrate the complexity of even a small number of sentences of 'real' English. To parse just the first six sentences of this famous story would require a considerably more complex grammar than the one we have developed so far, which would take us far outside the scope of this book.

Sadly we will go back to much simpler examples and use a file *sentences.txt* containing five sentences that are valid with the grammar defined in Section 12.2 and one sentence (the third) that is invalid.

```
[the,large,green,men,see,a,small,blue,dog].
[the,large,green,men,will_see,a,small,blue,dog].
[the,man].
[the,green,small,men,see,a,blue,dog].
[the,green,small,men,took,a,blue,dog].
[the,green,small,man,sees].
```

To process this file we need to add just a few lines to the program for analyzing sentences given at the end of Section 12.2. The second clause of predicate **proc2** enables us to trap the case where a list of words is not a valid sentence, at least as far as the grammar we have defined is concerned.

```
process(File):-
    see(File),repeat,read(S),proc(S),S=end_of_file,!,
    seen.

proc(end_of_file).
proc(S):-write('Sentence: '),write(S),nl,proc2(S).

proc2(S):-phrase(sentence(L1),S),write('Structure: '),
    write(L1),nl,nl,!.
proc2(S):-write('Invalid sentence structure'),nl,nl.
```

?-process('sentences.txt').
Sentence: [the,large,green,men,see,a,small,blue,dog]
Structure: [s2,plural,see,np1,men,np1,dog]

Sentence: [the,large,green,men,will_see,a,small,blue,dog]
Structure: [s1,both,will_see,np1,men,np1,dog]

Sentence: [the,man]
Invalid sentence structure

Sentence: [the,green,small,men,see,a,blue,dog]
Structure: [s2,plural,see,np1,men,np1,dog]

Sentence: [the,green,small,men,took,a,blue,dog]
Structure: [s1,both,took,np1,men,np1,dog]

Sentence: [the,green,small,man,sees]
Structure: [s4,singular,sees,np1,man]

true.

Chapter Summary

This chapter describes the use of the special syntax provided in Prolog for analyzing grammar rules: the operator $->/2$, the predicate **phrase/2** and braces to enclose 'regular' Prolog used in conjunction with grammar rules. A simple grammar able to deal with basic sentences is defined. Predicates are given to enable the validity of sentences presented as lists of words to be established and to extract important information such as the type of each *noun_phrase* from valid sentences. Finally, predicates are defined to convert sentences in standard English into the 'list of words' form required by the grammar rules.

Practical Exercise 12

Extend the grammar rules given at the end of Section 12.2 to allow for the possibility of an adverb at the end of a sentence of type s3 or s4. Define the following words as adverbs: well, badly, quickly, slowly.

Chapter 13
Prolog in Action

Chapter Aims

After reading this chapter you should be able to:

- Implement an artificial language of your own devising, using the techniques described elsewhere in this book. This will be illustrated by a simple language to control the movements of an imaginary robot.
- Implement a shell program, which can be used to construct a series of similar applications (the example used is a series of multiple-choice tests or quizzes). There are two phases to the implementation: the setup phase, during which the 'content' of the application is read in from a data file and converted into facts placed in the Prolog database, and the execution phase where a dialogue with the user is automatically generated.

13.1   Implementing an Artificial Language

This chapter continues the theme of the previous one by illustrating how Prolog can be used to implement applications of an 'Artificial Intelligence' kind. We will illustrate two such areas: the first is a program to control an imaginary robot; the second is an Expert System Shell for use in constructing and delivering multiple-choice tests or quizzes.

We start by developing a very simple language for controlling the movements of an imaginary robot and will show how it can be implemented in Prolog using a simplified version of the methods shown in Chapter 12.

M. Bramer, *Logic Programming with Prolog*, DOI 10.1007/978-1-4471-5487-7_13,
© Springer-Verlag London 2013

We will imagine that initially the robot is at the origin of two axes running from West to East and from North to South.

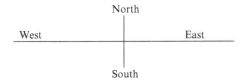

We will refer to its position in terms of the number of metres North and East of that position (the values may both be negative, indicating South and/or West of the starting point).

Initially the robot is facing North. It can turn either clockwise or anti-clockwise to an unlimited extent, but we will always refer to its orientation as a number of degrees anticlockwise from East, so initially the orientation is 90 degrees.

For convenience (and without any loss of generality) we will restrict the value of the orientation of the robot to the range of numbers from zero to (just less than) 360. Thus 390 degrees will be adjusted to 30 degrees and -10 degrees will become 350 degrees etc.

The aim is to enable the user to control the robot using a sequence of commands such as the following, ending with 'stop'. For convenience we will allow all commands to use lower case and upper case letters interchangeably. Commands will be written without surrounding quotes and with no final full stops.

```
forward 6 metres
turn right
turn left
turn 30 degrees clockwise
TURN Left
back 5 metres
turn ROUND
turn 60 degrees anticlockwise
report
goto 63 north 25 east
FACE 90 degrees
Stop
```

The following table shows the commands available in the very restricted language available for controlling our robot and the effect of acting on each one. We use *n* and *m* to indicate any numbers.

TURN n degrees anticlockwise	Add n to current orientation
TURN n degrees clockwise	Equivalent to 'TURN -n degrees anticlockwise'
TURN RIGHT	Equivalent to 'TURN -90 degrees anticlockwise'
TURN LEFT	Equivalent to 'TURN 90 degrees anticlockwise'
TURN ROUND	Equivalent to 'TURN 180 degrees anticlockwise'
FORWARD n metres	Go forward n metres using current orientation
BACK n metres	Equivalent to 'TURN ROUND' and then 'FORWARD n metres'
GOTO n North m East	Change position to n metres North and m metres East
FACE n degrees	Change orientation to n degrees (anticlockwise from East)
REPORT	State current position and orientation
STOP	REPORT and then stop

We can write a basic program to read in a sequence of lines one at a time and write them out again until a line containing just STOP is input as follows:

```
go:-repeat,inputline([],L),name(S,L),write('S='),
    write(S),nl,
    S='STOP',write('FINISHED'),nl.

inputline(OldL,L):-get0(X),process(X,OldL,L).

process(10,L,L).
process(X,OldL,NewL):-
    X=\=10,append(OldL,[X],L2),inputline(L2,NewL).
```

?- go.
|: FORWARD 6 metres
S=FORWARD 6 metres
|: TURN RIGHT
S=TURN RIGHT
|: TURN LEFT
S=TURN LEFT
|: STOP
S=STOP
FINISHED
true .

However this does not get us very far. The first improvement we need is to incorporate some of the code developed in Chapter 12.3 to convert each line input into a 'list of words' form and to write it out again. (This may not seem like a valuable advance but it will turn out to be one, as will be shown later.)

Unlike the conversion of English sentences to list form in Section 12.3, for this application the end of an input line is marked by a character with ASCII value 10, not a full stop, exclamation mark or question mark. Also we do not need to allow for any separators between words except spaces. Finally as we will be inputting commands for the robot at the console not via a text file there is no possibility of encountering an end of file character (ASCII value -1).

These considerations lead to the following revised program.

```
control_robot:-repeat,inputline(L),L=[stop],!.

inputline(L):-buildlist(L,[]),reverse(L,L1),
    writeout(L1),!.

writeout([""]).
writeout(L):-writeq(L),nl.

buildlist(L,OldL):-findword(Word,[]),
(
    (Word=[],L=OldL);
    (Word=[sep],buildlist(L,OldL));
    (Word=[termin|Word1],name(S,Word1),L=[S|OldL]);
    (name(S,Word),buildlist(L,[S|OldL]))
).

findword(Word,OldWord):-get0(X1),repchar(X1,X),
(
    (terminator(X),Word=[termin|OldWord]);
    (separator(X),((OldWord=[],Word=[sep]);
    Word=OldWord));
    (append(OldWord,[X],New),findword(Word,New))
).

separator(32). /* space*/

terminator(10). /* end of line */

repchar(X,New):-X>=65,X=<90,New is X+32,!.
repchar(Char,Char).
```

?- control_robot.
|: back 8 metres
[back,8,metres]
|: TURN left
[turn,left]
|:
|: TURN right
[turn,right]

|: FORWARD 4 metres
[forward,4,metres]
|: STOP
[stop]
true.

Note that the program automatically ignores any blank lines. This is a consequence of the first clause of the **writeout** predicate. Note also that all the input has been converted automatically to lower case.

We will temporarily ignore the question of how the system should deal with invalid lines, which are probably most likely to be caused by typing errors. We want to avoid the robot control program crashing when that happens as far as possible.

The great benefit gained by the effort expended to get the input commands into the list of words format, one list per line of input, is that we can now use the 'univ' operator $=../2$ which was introduced in Chapter 11.

If we have a list L, say *[write,'Hello World']*, then evaluating the goal $X=..L$ will bind X to the term **write('Hello World')**. This term can then be evaluated as if it were a goal using the **call/1** predicate, which was also introduced in Chapter 11. For example:

?- L=[write,'Hello World'],G=..L,call(G).
Hello World
L = [write, 'Hello World'],
G = write('Hello World').

To take advantage of this for our application we can start by changing the **writeout** predicate to

```
writeout(["]).
writeout(L):-writeq(L),nl,X=..L,write(X),nl.
```

So that the list of words L is converted to a term X which is then printed out.

?- control_robot.
|: back 8 metres
[back,8,metres]
back(8,metres)
|: TURN left
[turn,left]
turn(left)
|:
|: TURN right
[turn,right]
turn(right)
|: FORWARD 4 metres
[forward,4,metres]

forward(4,metres)
|: STOP
[stop]
stop
true.

In order to make our robot program work, we now need to define predicates **turn**, **forward**, **report** etc. and then apply the **call** predicate to each of the terms obtained by converting lines of input, e.g. *back(8,metres)*, in turn. We can do the latter part by changing the definition of **writeout** to:

```
writeout([""]).
writeout(L):-writeq(L),nl,X=..L,write(X),nl,call(X).
```

Before defining the predicates **forward**, **turn** etc. we will first define a predicate for stopping the input loop:

```
stop:-write('End of Input '),nl.
```

?- control_robot.
|: STOP
[stop]
stop
End of Input
true.

As we have not yet defined any of the predicates **forward**, **turn** etc. apart from **stop**, the program as modified above is sure to fail as soon as anything else is input. This seems a good time to include some code to handle invalid input.

We can define a new predicate **verify/1** by

```
verify([H|L]):-
    member(H, [forward,back,turn,goto,face,
    report,stop]).
```

We can then change the definition of **writeout** to:

```
writeout([""]).
writeout(L):-writeq(L),nl,
    ((verify(L),X=..L,write(X),nl,call(X));
    (write('Invalid input'),nl)).
```

If the first element of list *L* is one of the atoms *forward*, *back*, *turn*, *goto*, *face*, *report* and *stop* we go on to convert the list to a term using '**univ**' and then call it. If the first element is anything else an error message is output. In either case the expanded form of the goal succeeds.

With these changes to our program we can now get output such as the following.

?- control_robot.
|: BBACK 6 metres
[bback,6,metres]
Invalid input
|: STOP
[stop]
stop
End of Input
true.

It remains to define the predicates **forward, back, turn, goto, face** and **report**. Before doing this we first need to decide how to store the robot's position (measured in metres North and East of the starting point) and its orientation (measured in degrees anticlockwise from East). A simple way of doing this is to place two clauses in the database:

- one for predicate **position/2**, where the first and second arguments correspond to the distance of the robot in metres from its starting point, in the North and East direction, respectively
- another for predicate **orientation/1**, where the argument corresponds to the number of degrees measured anticlockwise from East.

Initially we need to place the two clauses **position(0,0)** and **orientation(90)** in the database. This can be achieved by defining a new predicate **initialise/0** as:

```
initialise:-
  retractall(orientation(_)),
    retractall(position(_,_)),assertz(position(0,0)),
    /* zero metres North and zero metres East */
    assertz(orientation(90)).
    /* degrees anticlockwise from east*/
```

and changing the definition of **control_robot** to:

```
control_robot:-initialise,repeat,inputline(L),
    L=[stop],!.
```

We now turn to defining the **turn** predicate. There are five forms of *turn* command, the first four of which can be defined in terms of the last.

```
turn(right):-turn(90,degrees,clockwise).
turn(left):-turn(90,degrees,anticlockwise).
turn(round):-turn(180,degrees,anticlockwise).
   turn(N,degrees,clockwise):-N1 is -1*N,
   turn(N1,degrees,anticlockwise).
```

Turning *N* degrees anticlockwise is just a matter of adding *N* to the current orientation. We can do this by defining:

```
turn(N,degrees,anticlockwise):-retract(orientation
   (Current)),
   New is (Current+N) mod 360,assertz(orientation
   (New)),
   write('** New orientation is '),write(New),
   write(' degrees anticlockwise from East'),nl.
```

The reason for the term *(Current+N) mod 360* is to ensure that the angle is given in the 'standard' range for angles, i.e. as a number of degrees from 0 to (just less than) 360.

The FACE command simply involves retracting whatever **orientation** clause is currently in the database and asserting a new value.

```
face(N,degrees):-
  retract(orientation(_)),
  assertz(orientation(N)),
  write('** New orientation is '),
  write(N),write('degrees anticlockwise from East'),nl.
```

We can now tell the robot to turn (change its orientation) in six different ways. The next step is to define the **report** predicate, which writes out both the robot's position and its orientation.

```
report:-position(North,East),write('** Position is '),
    round2dp(North,North1),round2dp(East,East1),
    write(North1),
    write(' metres North and '),write(East1),
```

```
    write(' metres East'),nl,
    orientation(N),write('** Orientation is '),write(N),
    write(' degrees anticlockwise from East'),nl.

round2dp(X,Y):-Y is round(X*100)/100.
```

The **round2dp** predicate is used to round the distance in each direction to 2 decimal places before it is displayed.

We will also change the definition of **control_robot** to produce an automatic report immediately after initialisation.

```
control_robot:-
    initialise,report,repeat,inputline(L),L=[stop],!.
```

and simplify the definition of **writeout** to remove output that is no longer needed.

```
writeout(["]).
writeout(L):-((verify(L),X=..L,call(X));
    (write('Invalid input'),nl)).
```

With all these changes we can now produce the following dialogue with the robot control system.

?- control_robot.
** Position is 0 metres North and 0 metres East
** Orientation is 90 degrees anticlockwise from East
|: TURN right
** New orientation is 0 degrees anticlockwise from East
|: TURN 30 degrees clockwise
** New orientation is 330 degrees anticlockwise from East
|: TURN round
** New orientation is 150 degrees anticlockwise from East
|: TURN LEFT
** New orientation is 240 degrees anticlockwise from East
|: TURN 140 degrees anticlockwise
** New orientation is 20 degrees anticlockwise from East
|: REPORT
** Position is 0 metres North and 0 metres East
** Orientation is 20 degrees anticlockwise from East
|: FACE 70 degrees

** New orientation is 70 degrees anticlockwise from East
|: STOP
End of Input
true.

The predicates not yet defined are **forward**, **back** and **goto**.

Next we define the **goto** predicate, which instructs the robot to go to position *North* metres North and *East* metres East of its original starting point and then to adopt its previous orientation.

```
goto(North,north,East,east):-
    retract(position(_,_)),
    assertz(position(North,East)),
    write('** New position is '),
    write(North),
    write(' metres North and '),write(East),
    write(' metres East'),nl.
```

We will define the **back** predicate using **turn** and **forward**. To go back n metres, turn round and then go forward n metres.

```
back(N,metres):-
    turn(180,degrees,anticlockwise),forward(N,metres).
```

This just leaves the **forward** predicate to define.

If a robot goes forward *n* metres at an orientation of *d* degrees anticlockwise from the East direction, basic trigonometry tells us that it will travel *n x sin(d)* metres North and *n x cos(d)* metres East. These formulae apply for all values of *d*, even when they make one or both of the distances negative.[1]

However there is a complication in using these formulae and they need adjusting. So far in this section we have measured all the angles in degrees whereas the Prolog cosine and sine functions assume that angles are measured in radians.[2] Measuring angles in radians, although familiar to Mathematicians, is far less well-known to the general public (we will not attempt to justify it here). However it is easy to convert

---

[1] Readers unfamiliar with trigonometry will lose nothing by taking these formulae (and those that follow) on trust. This is a book about Prolog, not trigonometry.

[2] Warning – some versions of Prolog may measure angles in degrees not radians. To check which form of measurement applies to the version of Prolog you are using, enter a query such as

?-X is sin(90).

If a value of 1 is returned for X, angles are measured in degrees. If the value returned is approximately 0.894 then angles are measured in radians, as is assumed in the main text in this section.

from one to the other using the conversion formula π *radians = 180 degrees*. The Greek letter π (pronounced 'pi') is a well known 'mathematical constant', with approximate value 3.14159265. To calculate the distance measured in the north and east directions when moving forward *n* metres at an orientation of *d* degrees anticlockwise from east, we can use the formulae n *x sin(d x 3.14159265/180)* and *n x cos(d x 3.14159265/180)*, respectively. This leads to the following definition of predicate **forward**:

```
forward(N,metres):-
    retract(position(North,East)),
    orientation(Degrees),radians(Degrees,Rads),
    North1 is North+N*sin(Rads),
    East1 is East+N*cos(Rads),
    assertz(position(North1,East1)),
    write('** New position is '),
    round2dp(North1,North2),round2dp(East1,East2),
    write(North2),write(' metres North and '),
    write(East2),write(' metres East'),nl.

radians(N,M):-M is (3.14159265)*N/180.
/* N degrees converted to M radians
   (pi radians=180 degrees) */
```

Putting together all the Prolog clauses defined in the section we now have a complete program for our robot controller.

```
control_robot:-initialise,report,repeat,inputline(L),
    L=[stop],!.

inputline(L):-buildlist(L,[]),reverse(L,L1),
    writeout(L1),!.

writeout(['']).
writeout(L):-((verify(L),X=..L,call(X));
    (write('Invalid input'),nl)).

buildlist(L,OldL):-findword(Word,[]),
(
    (Word=[],L=OldL);
    (Word=[sep],buildlist(L,OldL));
    (Word=[termin|Word1],name(S,Word1),L=[S|OldL]);
    (name(S,Word),buildlist(L,[S|OldL]))
).
```

```
findword(Word,OldWord):-get0(X1),repchar(X1,X),
(
    (terminator(X),Word=[termin|OldWord]);
    (separator(X),((OldWord=[],Word=[sep]);
      Word=OldWord));
    (append(OldWord,[X],New),findword(Word,New))
).
separator(32). /* space*/

terminator(10). /* end of line */

repchar(X,New):-X>=65,X=<90,New is X+32,!.
repchar(Char,Char).

stop:-write('End of Input'),nl.

verify([H|L]):-
  member(H,[forward,back,turn,goto,face,report,stop]).

forward(N,metres):-
    retract(position(North,East)),
    orientation(Degrees),radians(Degrees,Rads),
    North1 is North+N*sin(Rads),
    East1 is East+N*cos(Rads),
    assertz(position(North1,East1)),
    write('** New position is '),
    round2dp(North1,North2),round2dp(East1,East2),
    write(North2),write(' metres North and '),
    write(East2),write(' metres East'),nl.

back(N,metres):-
    turn(180,degrees,anticlockwise),forward(N,metres).

turn(right):-turn(90,degrees,clockwise).
turn(left):-turn(90,degrees,anticlockwise).
turn(round):-turn(180,degrees,anticlockwise).
turn(N,degrees,clockwise):-N1 is -1*N,
    turn(N1,degrees,anticlockwise).
turn(N,degrees,anticlockwise):-retract(orientation
    (Current)),
    New is (Current+N) mod 360,assertz(orientation
    (New)),
    write('** New orientation is '),write(New),
```

```
        write(' degrees anticlockwise from East'),nl.

  goto(North,north,East,east):-
      retract(position(_,_)),
      assertz(position(North,East)),
      write('** New position is '),
      write(North),write(' metres North and '),
      write(East),write(' metres East'),nl.

  report:-position(North,East),write('** Position is '),
      round2dp(North,North1),round2dp(East,East1),
      write(North1),write(' metres North and '),
      write(East1),write(' metres East'),nl,
      orientation(N),write('** Orientation is '),write(N),
      write(' degrees anticlockwise from East'),nl.

  face(N,degrees):-
      retract(orientation(_)),
      assertz(orientation(N)),
      write('** New orientation is '),
    write(N),write('degrees anticlockwise from East'),nl.

  stop:-write('STOP'),nl,report.

  radians(N,M):-M is (3.14159265)*N/180.
  /* N degrees converted to M radians
  (pi radians=180 degrees) */

  round2dp(X,Y):-Y is round(X*100)/100.

  initialise:-
      retractall(orientation(_)),retractall
      (position(_,_)),
      assertz(position(0,0)),
      /* zero metres North and zero metres East */
      assertz(orientation(90)).
      /* degrees anticlockwise from east*/
```

?- control_robot.
** Position is 0 metres North and 0 metres East
** Orientation is 90 degrees anticlockwise from East
|: TURN 30 degrees clockwise
** New orientation is 60 degrees anticlockwise from East

|: **forward 10 metres**
** New position is 8.66 metres North and 5 metres East
|: **back 10 metres**
** New orientation is 240 degrees anticlockwise from East
** New position is 0 metres North and 0 metres East
|: **turn round**
** New orientation is 60 degrees anticlockwise from East
|: **report**
** Position is 0 metres North and 0 metres East
** Orientation is 60 degrees anticlockwise from East
|: **stop**
End of Input
true.

13.2 Developing an Expert System Shell

In this section we will change to a different 'Artificial Intelligence'-like application. We will start by imagining that we wish to develop a program to administer a multiple-choice test, score the user's replies and give the user feedback on his or her performance. Tests of this kind are commonplace in education, but they are also commonly seen in magazines and elsewhere as 'assess yourself' quizzes, often with remarkably simple questions. The example we use in this section will be a quiz of this 'less than difficult' kind. The essential point, however, is that we do not want to program just one quiz. We want to implement a framework in which a potentially large number of quizzes of the same kind can conveniently be made available to users.

This implies constructing a framework which is independent of the content of any particular quiz, with each specific quiz being read in and assembled automatically from a data file. This style of program is known as a *shell* or often as an *expert system shell*.

There are typically two phases to using a shell:

- The setup phase, during which the 'content' of the application (the quiz questions and answers etc.) are read in from a data file (a text file) and converted into facts placed in the Prolog database by using the **assertz** predicate.
- The execution phase where a dialogue with the user is automatically generated.

The Prolog program comprising the shell should be as general as possible. Although we cannot entirely avoid taking into account that the application is a multiple-choice quiz/test we should avoid building assumptions into our shell such as that there are always eight questions or that questions always have three possible answers.

The key to programming a shell of this kind is to start by envisaging the content of the data file for one specific application (quiz) and the Prolog facts corresponding to the data that need to be generated and placed in the database during the setup phase for that specific application. Once this design is done, the implementation often follows naturally.

Here is the content of a data file for a particularly easy multiple-choice quiz, which we will assume is stored in text file *quiz1.txt*.

'Are you a genius? Answer our quiz and find out!'.

'What is the name of this planet?'.
'Earth'. 20. 'The Moon'. 5. 'John'. 0. end.

'What is the capital of Great Britain?'.
'America'. 0. 'Paris'. 6. 'London'. 50. 'Moscow'. 4. end.

'In which country will you find the Sydney Opera House?'.
'London'. 5. 'Toronto'. 4. 'The Moon'. 2. 'Australia'. 10. 'Germany'. 8. end.

endquestions.

0. 20. 'You are definitely not a genius'.
21. 60. 'You need to do some more reading'.
61. 80. 'You are a genius!'.
endmarkscheme.

The data file comprises:

- The title of the quiz.
- The details of three questions and their possible answers followed by the term **endquestions**.

    For each question we have:

    The text of the question.
    Pairs of values terminated by end. Each pair comprises a possible answer followed by the number of marks to be awarded for it.

- A mark scheme (the lowest and highest values of a number of ranges of marks, each associated with a piece of feedback to the user) followed by **endmarkscheme**.

Note that in this example the input is given as a sequence of Prolog terms, each enclosed by quotes where required, terminated by a full stop and separated by one or more spaces or newline characters. (All the blank lines in the data file will be ignored.) All this is purely a matter of convenience (or otherwise) – the user will not see the data file.

During the setup phase the following Prolog clauses (all facts) will be generated from the data file and placed in the database using **assertz**.

```
title ('Are you a genius? Answer our quiz and find out!').

question ('What is the name of this planet?',
[ans ('Earth', 20), ans ('The Moon', 5), ans ('John', 0)], 20).

question ('What is the  capital of England?',
[ans ('America', 0), ans ('Paris', 6), ans ('London', 50),
ans ('Moscow', 4)], 50).

question ('In which country will you find the Sydney
    Opera House?',
[ans ('London', 5), ans ('Toronto', 4), ans ('The Moon', 2),
ans ('Australia', 10), ans ('Germany', 8)], 10).

range (0, 20, 'You are definitely not a genius').
range (21, 60, 'You need to do some more reading').
range (61, 80, 'You are a genius!').
```

There are three predicates shown above: **title**, **question** and **range**. The first is straightforward: the argument of **title/1** is the title of the quiz. The use of the **range/3** predicate should also be clear: each clause holds the lower and upper values of a range of potential scores obtained from answering the quiz together with the feedback to give the user if a score in that range is obtained.

There are three clauses (facts) for predicate **question**, one per question. Each one has three components:

- The question itself.
- A list of terms of the form *ans(Ans,Score)*, one for each possible answer to the question, *Ans*, with the second argument being the corresponding number of points, *Score*, that will be awarded for giving that answer.
- The maximum number of points available to be awarded for the question.

The last of these could have been included in the data file, but instead we will obtain it from the scores associated with each possible answer to a question, by taking the largest value.

These considerations lead directly to the following program to read in a data file, say *quiz1.txt*, and write a number of facts into the Prolog database.

```
setup:-
see('quiz1.txt'),readin,seen,write('Setup completed'),nl.

readin:-read(Title),assertz(title(Title)),readqs.

readqs:-repeat,read(Qtext),process(Qtext),
   Qtext=endquestions,readranges.

process(endquestions):-!.

process(Qtext):-proc2([],Anslist,-9999,Maxscore),
   assertz(question(Qtext,Anslist,Maxscore)).

proc2(Anscurrent,Anslist,Maxsofar,Maxscore):
   -read(Ans),
(
   (Ans=end,Anslist=Anscurrent,Maxscore=Maxsofar,!);
   (read(Score),append(Anscurrent,[ans(Ans,Score)],
   Ansnew),Maxnew is max(Maxsofar,Score),
   proc2(Ansnew,Anslist,Maxnew,Maxscore))
).

readranges:-
   repeat,read(First),proc(First),First=endmarkscheme.

proc(endmarkscheme):-!.
proc(First):-read(Last),read(Feedback),
   assertz(range(First,Last,Feedback)).
```

The definition of predicate **readranges** is typical of the way that a shell of this kind can be constructed using **repeat** loops of the kind introduced in Chapter 6. We read a value for term *First* (the lower bound of the next range), process it, then go back and read another value for *First*, and so on, continuing until the value **endmarkscheme** in found. 'Processing' the value of *First* (using predicate **proc**) either means doing nothing with it, if it is the term **endmarkscheme**, or otherwise reading two more terms, *Last* and *Feedback*, and combining them with *First* to form a **range/3** term that is then added to the Prolog database with **assertz**.

The processing of a question (using predicate **process**) is rather more complicated. The **process** predicate uses predicate **proc2** to read in pairs of possible answers and associated scores and place them in a list *Anslist*, while finding the highest possible score for the question and giving that value to variable *Maxscore*. This is handled by giving **proc2** four arguments:

- The answer/score list created so far (initially the empty list).
- The variable to which the final version of the list will be bound, i.e. *Anslist*.

- The highest score found so far for any answer to the question (initially -9999, which is chosen to be far below any value that is ever likely to be used in a real quiz).
- The variable to which the final version of the highest score will be bound, i.e. *Maxscore*.

After **proc2** reads each potential answer it checks whether it is the term *end*.

- If it is, it binds *Anslist*, the final version of the answer/score list, to whatever is its current version and also binds *Maxscore*, the final value of the highest score, to whatever is its current estimate.
- If not, it reads another term, giving the value of a new score, adds a new **ans/2** term, i.e. a new answer/score pair, to its current list of pairs (first argument), revises its value of the largest score found so far (third argument) and calls itself recursively to continue the process.

Having implemented the setup process, the next step for the developer is to envisage a typical user dialogue with the system. One possibility is that it should look like this:

Are you a genius? Answer our quiz and find out!

What is the name of this planet?
Possible answers are Earth, The Moon, and John
Enter your answer
|: The Moon
You have scored 5 points out of a possible 20

What is the capital of England?
Possible answers are America, Paris, London, and Moscow
Enter your answer
|: Moscow
You have scored 4 points out of a possible 50

In which country will you find the Sydney Opera House?
Possible answers are London, Toronto, The Moon, Australia, and Germany
Enter your answer
|: Toronto
You have scored 4 points out of a possible 10

Your total score is 13 points out of a possible 80

You are definitely not a genius

Note that although it is not essential it seems very desirable that the user's input should take the form of strings of characters not Prolog terms. There are several ways in which a **readline** facility can be implemented. One suitable for this application is given below:

```
readline(S):-readline2([],L),name(S,L),!.

readline2(Lcurrent,Lfinal):-get0(X),
  ((X=10,Lfinal=Lcurrent);
  (append(Lcurrent,[X],Lnew),readline2(Lnew,Lfinal))).
```

Predicate **readline2** creates a list of ASCII values of characters entered by the user, prior to an end of line character (ASCII value 10) being entered. Then **readline** takes this list and converts it to a string of characters using the **name** predicate described in Chapter 10.

Based on the dialogue given above we now need to consider what additional facts need to be added to the database when the user works through the quiz. On inspection it turns out that the only information that needs to be updated and stored as each question is asked and answered in turn is the user's total score so far and the maximum score available for all the questions answered so far. These two values can be held (in that order) as the arguments of a single predicate **myscore/2**.

After the setup stage is complete the user needs a facility for running the quiz (possibly several times) and as the first steps (or very early steps) in doing this we should retract any **myscore/2** clauses there may already be in the database and place a clause **myscore(0,0)** in the database. We can do this by including in our program the two clauses.

retractall(myscore(_,_)),assertz(myscore(0,0)),

The first task for a program to run a quiz that has already been placed in the database is to obtain the title of the quiz and display it as a heading. This gives us an initial (and incomplete) version of a program.

```
runquiz:-
retractall(myscore(_,_)),assertz(myscore(0,0)),
title(T),write(T),nl,nl,
askq.
```

It remains to implement predicate **askq**, which asks the user each question in turn, gives a score for the first valid answer obtained and then goes on to ask more questions until all the questions are exhausted, at which time it displays the user's total score, the maximum score obtainable for the quiz and finally uses the range clauses in the database to display feedback to the user.

The basic structure to use for **askq** is that of 'backtracking with failure', described in Section 6.4. This gives an initial outline version of **askq** as follows:

```
askq:-question(Qtext,Anslist,Maxscore),
write(Qtext),nl,

/* Use Anslist to tell the user the possible answers.
Request an answer from the user until one of the
possible ones is given, then tell the user how many
points he/she has obtained for that answer.
*/
fail.

askq:-
/*
Obtain the user's total score and the maximum possible
number of marks available from the 'myscore/2'
predicate and tell them to the user. Then use the
'range' predicate to give the user feedback on his/her
overall performance and finish.
*/
 .
```

We can deal with the part 'Use *Anslist* to tell the user the possible answers' by adding the goals

```
write('Possible answers are '),genanswers(Anslist),
```

into the definition of **askq** and defining a new predicate **genanswers** to display all the possible answers:

```
genanswers([ans(A,_)]):-write('and '),write(A),nl,!.
genanswers([ans(A,_)|L]):-write(A),write(', '),
genanswers(L).
```

The second clause of **askq** (when there are no more questions to ask) is also straightforward to implement:

```
askq:-myscore(M,Maxtotal),
    write('Your total score is '),write(M),
    write('points'),
```

```
write(' out of a possible '),write(Maxtotal),nl,
range(First,Last,Feedback),M>=First,M=<Last,
write(Feedback),nl,nl,nl.
```

This just leaves the need to implement for the first clause of **askq** 'request an answer from the user until one of the possible ones is given, then tell the user how many points he/she has obtained for that answer'.

We add to the definition of the first clause of **askq** (just before the *fail* goal)

```
requestanswer(Anslist,Maxscore),
```

and define a new predicate **requestanswer**

```
requestanswer(Anslist,Maxscore):-
    write('Enter your answer'),nl,
    readline(Answer),
    (
    (member(ans(Answer,Score),Anslist),
        usescore(Score,Maxscore),!);
    (write('That is not a valid answer - try again!'),nl,
        requestanswer(Anslist,Maxscore))
).
```

The user is repeatedly asked to enter an answer until he/she gives one that is valid. This is determined by testing whether the answer, *Answer*, is one for which there is a term *ans(Answer,Score)* in the list *Anslist*. When a valid answer is given, the **usescore** predicate tells the user how many points have been awarded for the answer given and the maximum number of points available for the question, using the values of *Score* and *Maxscore*, respectively. It then updates the **myscore/2** predicate with the two arguments recording the total number of points awarded so far and the maximum number of points available for all questions answered so far, respectively

A suitable definition of **usescore/2** is as follows:

```
usescore(Score,Maxscore):-
 write('You have scored '),write(Score),write(' points'),
 write(' out of a possible '),write(Maxscore),nl,nl,
 retract(myscore(Old,Oldtotal)),
 New is Old+Score,Newtotal is Oldtotal+Maxscore,
 assertz(myscore(New,Newtotal)).
```

Putting all the code fragments in this section together we get a complete definition of a program that will administer a quiz previously converted into **title**, **question** and **range** clauses by the **setup** predicate given previously.

```prolog
runquiz:-
    retractall(myscore(_,_)),assertz(myscore(0,0)),
    title(T),write(T),nl,nl,
    askq.

askq:-question(Qtext,Anslist,Maxscore),
    write(Qtext),nl,
    write('Possible answers are '),genanswers(Anslist),
    requestanswer(Anslist,Maxscore),fail.

askq:-myscore(M,Maxtotal),
    write('Your total score is'),write(M),write('points'),
    write(' out of a possible '),write(Maxtotal),nl,
    range(First,Last,Feedback),M>=First,M=<Last,
    write(Feedback),nl,nl,nl.

genanswers([ans(A,_)]):-write('and '),write(A),nl,!.
genanswers([ans(A,_)|L]):-write(A),write(', '),
genanswers(L).

requestanswer(Anslist,Maxscore):-
    write('Enter your answer'),nl,
    readline(Answer),
    (
    (member(ans(Answer,Score),Anslist),
        usescore(Score,Maxscore),!);
    (write('That is not a valid answer - try again!'),nl,
        requestanswer(Anslist,Maxscore))
    ).

usescore(Score,Maxscore):-
    write('You have scored '),write(Score),
        write(' points'),
    write(' out of a possible '),write(Maxscore),nl,nl,
    retract(myscore(Old,Oldtotal)),
    New is Old+Score,Newtotal is Oldtotal+Maxscore,
    assertz(myscore(New,Newtotal)).

readline(S):-readline2([],L),name(S,L),!.
```

```
readline2(Lcurrent,Lfinal):-get0(X),
   ((X=10,Lfinal=Lcurrent);
   (append(Lcurrent,[X],Lnew),readline2(Lnew,Lfinal))).
```

?- runquiz.
Are you a genius? Answer our quiz and find out!

What is the name of this planet?
Possible answers are Earth, The Moon, and John
Enter your answer
|: John
You have scored 0 points out of a possible 20

What is the capital of Great Britain?
Possible answers are America, Paris, London, and Moscow
Enter your answer
|: London
You have scored 50 points out of a possible 50

In which country will you find the Sydney Opera House?
Possible answers are London, Toronto, The Moon, Australia, and Germany
Enter your answer
|: Toronto
You have scored 4 points out of a possible 10

Your total score is 54 points out of a possible 80
You need to do some more reading

true .

The **retractall** goal in the second line of the program makes it possible for the **runquiz** predicate to be used repeatedly either by the same user or by different users, without any need to reload the **title**, **question** and **range** predicates.

This section has illustrated a typical example of a shell. It comprises two separate programs: one to setup the data (i.e. to read in a data file, create a number of Prolog facts equivalent to the contents of the file and assert them to the Prolog database) and one to make use of the facts in the database. Once a shell has been created it is straightforward to create (in this case) a new quiz or multiple-choice test, simply by creating a new data file, say *quiz2.txt*, without any further programming being required.

Chapter Summary

This chapter illustrates how Prolog can be used to develop applications of an 'Artificial Intelligence' kind. It is shown how to implement (1) an artificial language to control the movements of an imaginary robot and (2) a shell program that can be used to construct a series of similar applications, in this case multiple-choice tests or quizzes.

Practical Exercise 13

Change the definition of the multiple-choice test/quiz shell so that the questions are numbered in sequence, e.g.

Question 1. What is the name of this planet?

Appendix 1
Built-in Predicates

This appendix gives a brief description of each built-in predicate mentioned in this book and some others. They are all 'standard' predicates, which should be available in every version of Prolog, but inevitably there may be some exceptions to this. It is also possible that in some implementations of Prolog the definitions may vary slightly from those given here. In cases of disagreement, the definitions given in the supplier's documentation should always be taken as definitive.

Name of Predicate **!/0** [exclamation mark symbol, pronounced 'cut']
Syntax !
Description
Always succeeds. Used to control backtracking (see Chapter 7).
Name of Predicate **append/1**
Syntax **append(Stream)**
Description
Similar to **tell/1** but whereas for **tell/1** any existing file with the same name is deleted, any existing file is not deleted and any output is placed after the end of the existing contents of the file (see Chapter 5). The predicate used for this may vary in different implementations of Prolog.
Name of Predicate **append/3**
Syntax **append(First,Second,Whole)**
Description
Join or split lists (see Chapter 9).
Name of Predicate **arg/3**
Syntax **arg(N,Term,Arg)**
Description
N must be a positive integer and Term must be a compound term. Arg is unified with the Nth argument of Term.

M. Bramer, *Logic Programming with Prolog*, DOI 10.1007/978-1-4471-5487-7, © Springer-Verlag London 2013

Name of Predicate **asserta/1**

Syntax **asserta(Clause)**

Description

Adds a clause to the definition of a predicate at the beginning of its sequence of existing clauses (if any).

Name of Predicate **assertz/1**

Syntax **assertz(Clause)**

Description

Adds a clause to the definition of a predicate at the end of its sequence of existing clauses (if any).

Name of Predicate **atom/1**

Syntax **atom(Term)**

Description

Succeeds if and only if the given Term is a Prolog atom.

Name of Predicate **atomic/1**

Syntax **atomic(Term)**

Description

Succeeds if and only if Term is an atom, a number, or a variable bound to either.

Name of Predicate **call/1**

Syntax **call(Goal)**

Description

Calls the given Goal. Succeeds if Goal succeeds and fails if Goal fails.

Name of Predicate **consult/1**

Syntax **consult(Filename)**

Description

Loads the program contained in the named disk file.

Name of Predicate **dynamic/1**

Syntax **dynamic(predicate_specification)**

Description

Used to specify that a predicate is 'dynamic', i.e. may be modified (see Chapter 8).

Name of Predicate **fail/0**

Syntax **fail**

Description

Always fails. Used to force a program to backtrack.

Name of Predicate **findall/3**

Syntax **findall(Term,Goal,List)**

Description

Returns a list of all the instances of Term that satisfy goal Goal.

Name of Predicate **functor/3**

Syntax **functor(Term,Functor,Arity)**

Description

Succeeds if Term has the specified Functor and Arity.

Name of Predicate **get/1**

Syntax **get(Char)**

Description

This reads the next 'printable' (i.e. non-white-space) character from the current input stream, and unifies Char with its integer character code.

Name of Predicate **get0/1**

Syntax **get0(Char)**

Description

This reads the next character from the current input stream, and unifies Char with its integer character code.

Name of Predicate **halt/0**

Syntax **halt**

Description

Terminates the current Prolog session and exits to the operating system.

Name of Predicate **integer/1**

Syntax **integer(Term)**

Description

Succeeds if and only if Term is an integer.

Name of Predicate **length/2**

Syntax **length(List,Length)**

Description

Tests the length of a list (see Chapter 9).

Name of Predicate **listing/1**

Syntax **listing(Atom)**

Description

Lists all predicates with the given name, irrespective of their arity.

Name of Predicate **member/2**

Syntax **member(Term,List)**

Description

Gets or checks a member of a list (see Chapter 9).

Name of Predicate **name/2**

Syntax **name(Atom,List)**

Description

Converts between an atom and a list of characters (see Chapter 10).

Name of Predicate **nl/0**

Syntax **nl**

Description

Outputs a carriage return and line feed to the current output stream, to complete a line of output.

Name of Predicate **op/3**

Syntax **op(Precedence,Type,Name)**

Description

Used to set, reset or clear the definition of an operator, using the given Precedence, Type and Name.

Name of Predicate **phrase/2**

Syntax **phrase(Syntactic Term, List of Words)**

Description

Satisfied if the list of words is a valid example of the syntactic term (see Chapter 12).

Name of Predicate **put/1**

Syntax **put(Integer)**

Description

Outputs the character corresponding to Integer to the current output stream.

Name of Predicate **read/1**

Syntax **read(Var)**

Description

Reads a term from the current input stream and attempts to assign the value to *Var*, which should previously be unbound.

Name of Predicate **repeat/0**

Syntax **repeat**

Description

Always succeeds when called, both when called and on backtracking. Used to provide a looping facility.

Name of Predicate **retract/1**

Syntax **retract(Clause)**

Description

Deletes the first matching clause from a predicate (see Chapter 8).

Name of Predicate **retractall/1**

Syntax retractall(Head)

Description

Deletes all clauses whose heads match the given Head (see Chapter 8).

Name of Predicate **reverse/2**

Syntax **reverse(List,Reverse)**

Description

Reverses the order of elements in a list (see Chapter 9).

Name of Predicate **see/1**

Syntax **see(Stream)**

Description

Sets Stream to be the current input stream. Stream may be the name of a disk file or the atom *user* (referring to the console input device). If Stream refers to a disk file which is not open, it is automatically opened for reading. If the file is already open, input continues from the point immediately after the previously-read character.

Name of Predicate **seeing/1**

Syntax **seeing(Stream)**

Description

Stream is bound to the name of the current input stream, which may be a disk file or the atom *user* (referring to the console input device).

Name of Predicate **seen/0**

Syntax **seen**

Description

Closes the file associated with the current input stream, and resets the current input stream to *user*.

Name of Predicate **statistics/0**

Syntax **statistics**

Description

Displays statistics about the current session.

Name of Predicate **tell/1**

Syntax **tell(Stream)**

Description

Sets the current output stream, which may be a disk file or the atom *user* (referring to the console output device). Any existing disk file with the same name is deleted. If the file is already open, output continues from the point immediately after the previously written character.

Name of Predicate **telling/1**

Syntax **telling(Stream)**

Description

Gets the current output Stream, which may be a disk file or the atom *user* (referring to the console output device). Stream is bound to the name of the current output stream.

Name of Predicate **told/0**

Syntax **told**

Description

Closes the file associated with the current output stream, and resets the current output stream to *user*.

Name of Predicate **true/0**

Syntax **true**

Description

Always succeeds.

Name of Predicate **write/1**

Syntax **write(Term)**

Description

Writes Term to the current output stream, in unquoted syntax.

Name of Predicate **writeq/1**

Syntax **writeq(Term)**

Description

Writes Term to the current output stream, in quoted syntax.

Appendix 2
Built-in Operators

This appendix gives a brief description of each built-in operator mentioned in this book and some others. They are all 'standard' operators, which should be available in every version of Prolog, but inevitably there may be some exceptions to this. It is also possible that in some implementations of Prolog the definitions may vary slightly from those given here. In cases of disagreement, the definitions given in the supplier's documentation should always be taken as definitive.

Name of Operator	, [comma]
Type of Operator	infix
Syntax	**Goal1,Goal2**
Description	
Succeeds if and only if Goal1 and Goal2 are both true.	
Name of Operator	; [semicolon]
Type of Operator	infix
Syntax	**Goal1;Goal2**
Description	
Succeeds if either Goal1 or Goal2 is true (or both).	
Name of Operator	=
Type of Operator	infix
Syntax	**Term1 = Term2**
Description	
Succeeds if terms Term1 and Term2 unify (see Chapter 4).	
Name of Operator	\=
Type of Operator	infix
Syntax	**Term\=Term2**
Description	
Succeeds if Term1 does not unify with Term2 (see Chapter 4).	

M. Bramer, *Logic Programming with Prolog*, DOI 10.1007/978-1-4471-5487-7,
© Springer-Verlag London 2013

Name of Operator ==

Type of Operator infix

Syntax **Term1 == Term2**

Description

Succeeds if Term1 is identical to Term2 (see Chapter 4).

Name of Operator \==

Type of Operator infix

Syntax **Term1 \== Term2**

Description

Succeeds if Term1 is not identical to Term2 (see Chapter 4).

Name of Operator =:=

Type of Operator infix

Syntax **Exp1 =:= Exp2**

Description

Succeeds if the arithmetic expressions Exp1 and Exp2 evaluate to the same numerical value (see Chapter 4).

Name of Operator =\=

Type of Operator infix

Syntax **Exp1 =\= Exp2**

Description

Succeeds if the arithmetic expressions Exp1 and Exp2 do not evaluate to the same numerical value (see Chapter 4).

Name of Operator =.. [pronounced 'univ']

Type of Operator infix

Syntax **Term=..List**

Description

Converts from a list to a term or vice versa (see Chapter 11).

Name of Operator <

Type of Operator infix

Syntax **Exp1<Exp2**

Description

Succeeds if the value of arithmetic expression Exp1 is less than the value of arithmetic expression Exp2.

Name of Operator =<

Type of Operator infix

Syntax **Exp1=<Exp2**

Description

Succeeds if the value of arithmetic expression Exp1 is less than or equal to the value of arithmetic expression Exp2.

Name of Operator >

Type of Operator infix

Syntax **Exp1>Exp2**

Description

Succeeds if the value of arithmetic expression Exp1 is greater than the value of arithmetic expression Exp2.

Name of Operator >=

Type of Operator infix

Syntax **Exp1>=Exp2**

Description

Succeeds if the value of arithmetic expression Exp1 is greater than or equal to the value of arithmetic expression Exp2.

Name of Operator ->

Type of Operator infix

Syntax **head->body** (in a grammar rule)

Description

Used in grammar rules (see Chapter 12).

Name of Operator **is/2**

Type of Operator infix

Syntax **Result is Expression**

Description

Expression must be a valid arithmetic expression which is evaluated to give a number. If Result is an unbound variable (the usual case) the variable is bound to the value of the expression. If Result is a bound variable with a numerical value or a number, the goal succeeds if the values of both sides of the **is** operator are the same and fails otherwise.

Name of Operator **not/1**

Type of Operator prefix

Syntax **not Goal**

Description

Succeeds if Goal fails, fails if Goal succeeds.

Note: in some versions of Prolog **not/1** is defined as a predicate with one argument but not as an operator. In such cases it can be made into an operator as shown in Section 4.4.

Appendix 3
Specimen Solutions to Practical Exercises

Practical Exercise 1

Question 2

A suitable program would comprise the five clauses:

```
animal(lion).
animal(tiger).
animal(cow).
carnivore(lion).
carnivore(tiger).
```

Suitable sequences of goals to test (a) to (d) are as follows.

?- animal(tiger).
true.

?- animal(cow),animal(tiger).
true.

?- animal(lion),carnivore(lion).
true.

?- animal(cow),carnivore(cow).
false.

M. Bramer, *Logic Programming with Prolog*, DOI 10.1007/978-1-4471-5487-7,
© Springer-Verlag London 2013

Question 3

Here is the output produced by one Prolog system for the specified goals, with explanations inserted in *italic*.

?- write(hello).
hello
true.
?- write(Hello).
_G884
true.

This obscure output is produced because Hello is not an atom (it begins with a capital letter). To print Hello World with a capital H it must be enclosed in quotes.

?- write('Hello!').
Hello!
true.

It is not (usually) possible to suppress the final 'true', which indicates that the goal has been satisfied. However the output can be made more readable by using 'nl' to generate a newline after 'Hello!' (if the Prolog system does not automatically provide one before it outputs 'true' or 'false').

?- write('Hello!'),nl.
Hello!
true.

?-100=100.
true.

?- 100=1000/10.
false.

Using $=$ is not the right way to do arithmetic – see Chapter 4.

?- 100 is 1000/10.
true.

?- 1000 is 100*10.
true.

?- 2 is (5+7)/6.
true.

?- 74 is (5+7)*6.
false.

Practical Exercise 2

Question 1

A suitable series of goals is as follows:

?- animal(mammal,A,_,_).
A = tiger;
A = hyena;
A = lion;
A = zebra

?- animal(mammal,A,carnivore,_).
A = tiger;
A = hyena;
A = lion;
false.

?- animal(mammal,A,_,stripes).
A = tiger;
A = zebra

?- animal(reptile,A,_,mane).
false.

Question 2

A suitable additional rule would be

```
couple(X,Y):-person(X,male),person(Y,female).
```

Testing this gives the following output:

?- couple(X,Y).
X = bill ,
Y = carol ;

X = bill ,
Y = margaret ;

X = bill ,
Y = jane ;

X = george ,
Y = carol ;

X = george ,
Y = margaret ;

X = george ,
Y = jane ;

X = alfred ,
Y = carol ;

X = alfred ,
Y = margaret ;

X = alfred ,
Y = jane

Practical Exercise 3

Question 1

Suitable definitions are given below:

```
child_of(A,B):-parent(B,A).
grandfather_of(A,B):-father(A,C),parent(C,B).
grandmother_of(A,B):-mother(A,C),parent(C,B).
great_grandfather_of(A,B):-
     father(A,C),grandfather_of(C,B).
great_grandfather_of(A,B):-
     father(A,C),grandmother_of(C,B).
```

?- child_of(X,ann).
X = henry ;
X = mary ;
false.

?- grandfather_of(A,caroline).
A = francis ;
false.

?- grandmother_of(B,caroline).
B = janice ;
false.

?- great_grandfather_of(C,caroline).
C = john ;
false.

Question 2

The system begins by matching the goal with the first clause defining the **ancestor/2** predicate, i.e. [A1].

```
                        ancestor(louise,Desc).

[A1]  ancestor(louise,Y):-parent(louise,Y).
```
X is bound to *louise*. Variables *Desc* and *Y* are bound to each other.

The goal **parent(louise,Y)** is now matched with clause [P3], which is first rewritten to replace *X* and *Y* by *X1* and *Y1*, i.e.

```
  parent(X1,Y1):-mother(X1,Y1).
```

```
                        ancestor(louise,Desc).

[A1]  ancestor(louise,Y):-parent(louise,Y).

[P3] parent(louise,Y1):-mother(louise,Y1).
```
X is bound to *louise*. Variables *Desc*, *Y* and *Y1* are bound to each other. *X1* is bound to *louise*.

The system now tries to satisfy the goal **mother(louise,Y1)**. It matches it with clause [M9].

```
                        ancestor(louise,Desc).

[A1]  ancestor(louise,Y):-parent(louise,Y).

[P3] parent(louise,Y1):-mother(louise,Y1).

[M9] mother(louise,caroline).
```
X is bound to *louise*. Variables *Desc*, *Y* and *Y1* are bound to each other and to *caroline*. *X1* is bound to *louise*.

This gives a solution to the user's goal, with *Desc* bound to *caroline*.

?- ancestor(louise,Desc).
Desc = caroline

If the user now forces the system to backtrack, the system will try to resatisfy the goal **mother(louise,Y1)** and fail. This will cause the rule [P3] to be rejected. Attempts to resatisfy **parent(louise,Y)** in the body of [A1] will also fail, so clause [A1] will be rejected. This brings the system back to the original goal **ancestor(louise,Desc)**.
The system tries to resatisfy it by matching it with the second clause for **ancestor/2**, i.e. [A2].

```
                        ancestor(louise,Desc).

[A2]  ancestor(louise,Y):-parent(louise,Z),ancestor(Z,Y).
```
X is bound to *louise*. Variables *Desc* and *Y* are bound to each other. Variable *Z* is unbound.

The system now tries to satisfy the goal parent(**louise,Z**). It matches it with [P3], which is first rewritten as (say)

parent(X1,Y1):-mother(X1,Y1).

```
                        ancestor(louise,Desc).

[A2]  ancestor(louise,Y):-parent(louise,Z),ancestor(Z,Y).

[P3] parent(louise,Y1):-mother(louise,Y1).
```
X is bound to *louise*. Variables *Desc* and *Y* are bound to each other. Variables *Y1* and *Z* are bound to each other. Variable *X1* is bound to *louise*.

It now tries to satisfy the goal **mother(louise,Y1)**. It matches it with clause [M9].

```
                        ancestor(louise,Desc).

[A2]  ancestor(louise,Y):-parent(louise,caroline),ancestor(caroline,Y).

[P3] parent(louise,caroline):-mother(louise,caroline).

[M9] mother(louise,caroline).
```
X is bound to *louise*. Variables *Desc* and *Y* are bound to each other. Variables *Z* any *Y1* are bound to each other and to *caroline*. Variable *X1* is bound to *louise*.

The next step is to satisfy the goal **ancestor(caroline,Y)**. It is matched with [A1], which is first rewritten as (say)

ancestor(X2,Y2):-parent(X2,Y2).

```
                        ancestor(louise,Desc).

[A2]  ancestor(louise,Y):-parent(louise,caroline),ancestor(caroline,Y).

[P3] parent(louise,caroline):-mother(louise,caroline).

[M9] mother(louise,caroline).

[A1] ancestor(X2,Y2):-parent(caroline,Y2).
```
X is bound to *louise*. Variables *Desc* and *Y* are bound to each other. Variables *Z* and *Y1* are bound to each other and to *caroline*. Variable *X1* is bound to *louise*. Variable *X2* is bound to *caroline*. Variables *Y* and *Y2* are bound to each other.

Next the system tries to satisfy **parent(caroline,Y2)**. It matches it with [P3], which is first rewritten as (say)

> parent(X3,Y3):-mother(X3,Y3).

---

ancestor(louise,Desc).

[A2] ancestor(louise,Y):-parent(louise,caroline),ancestor(caroline,Y).

[P3] parent(louise,caroline):-mother(louise,caroline).

[M9] mother(louise,caroline).

[A1] ancestor(X2,Y2):-parent(caroline,Y2).

[P3] parent(caroline,Y3):-mother(caroline,Y3).

X is bound to *louise*. Variables *Desc* and *Y* are bound to each other. Variables *Z* and *Y1* are bound to each other and to *caroline*. Variable *X1* is bound to *louise*. Variable *X2* is bound to *caroline*. Variables *Y*, *Y2* and *Y3* are bound to each other. *X3* is bound to *caroline*.

Next the system tries to satisfy **mother(caroline,Y3)**. It matches it with [M10].

---

ancestor(louise,Desc).

[A2] ancestor(louise,Y):-parent(louise,caroline),ancestor(caroline,david).

[P3] parent(louise,caroline):-mother(louise,caroline).

[M9] mother(louise,caroline).

[A1] ancestor(X2,david):-parent(caroline,david).

[P3] parent(caroline,david):-mother(caroline,david).

[M10] mother(caroline,david).

X is bound to *louise*. Variables *Desc* and *Y* are bound to each other. Variables *Z* any *Y1* are bound to each other and to *caroline*. Variable *X1* is bound to *louise*. Variable *X2* is bound to *caroline*. *X3* is bound to *caroline*. Variables *Y* , *Y2* and *Y3* are bound to each other and to *david*.

Now all the goals in the body of [A2] have succeeded, so the original goal **ancestor(louise,Desc)** succeeds with *Desc* bound to *david*.

Another solution with *Desc* bound to *janet* is available by backtracking.

?- ancestor(louise,Desc).
Desc = caroline ;
Desc = david ;
Desc = janet ;
false.

Practical Exercise 4

Question 1

The following program is a possible solution. There is no need to change the names of the predicates to **isa_dog** etc., but it makes the program easier to read if you do.

```
?-op(150,xf,isa_dog).
?-op(150,xf,isa_cat).
?-op(150,xf,is_large).
?-op(150,xf,is_small).
?-op(150,xf,isa_large_dog).
?-op(150,xf,isa_small_animal).
?-op(150,xfy,chases).
fido isa_dog. fido is_large.
mary isa_cat. mary is_large.
rover isa_dog. rover is_small.
jane isa_cat. jane is_small.
tom isa_dog. tom is_small.
harry isa_cat.
fred isa_dog. fred is_large.
henry isa_cat. henry is_large.
bill isa_cat.
steve isa_cat. steve is_large.
jim is_large.
mike is_large.
X isa_large_dog:- X isa_dog,X is_large.
A isa_small_animal:- A isa_dog,A is_small.
B isa_small_animal:- B isa_cat,B is_small.
X chases Y:-
     X isa_large_dog,Y isa_small_animal,
     write(X),write(' chases '),write(Y),nl.
```

There are six possible ways of satisfying the goal **X chases Y.**

?- X chases Y.
fido chases rover
X = fido ,
Y = rover ;

fido chases tom
X = fido ,
Y = tom ;

fido chases jane
X = fido ,
Y = jane ;

fred chases rover
X = fred ,
Y = rover ;

fred chases tom
X = fred ,
Y = tom ;

fred chases jane
X = fred ,
Y = jane ;

false.

Question 2

A possible definition is given below.

```
pred(A,B):-X is (A+B)/2,write('Average is: '),
write(X),nl,Y is sqrt(A*B),
write('Square root of product is: '),write(Y),nl,
Z is max(X,Y),write('Larger is: '),write(Z),nl.
```

?- pred(6,7).
Average is: 6.5
Square root of product is: 6.48074069840786
Larger is: 6.5
true.

?- pred(1,9).
Average is: 5
Square root of product is: 3.0
Larger is: 5
true.

Practical Exercise 5

Question 1

A possible definition is as follows:

```
makelower:-get0(X),process(X).
process(10):-nl.
process(X):-X=\=10,convert(X,Y),put(Y),makelower.
convert(X,Y):-X>=65,X=<90,Y is X+32.
convert(X,X):-X<65.
convert(X,X):-X>90.
```

Question 2

```
copyterms(Infile,Outfile):-
    seeing(S),telling(T),
    see(Infile),tell(Outfile),
    copy,
    seen,see(S),told,tell(T).
copy:-read(X),process(X).
process(end_of_file).
process(X):-
    X\=end_of_file,
    writeq(X),write('.'),nl,copy.
```

Note the use of write('.') to output a full stop after each term, so that the file may subsequently be read in again as specified.

Question 3

A possible definition of **readfile** is given below.

```
readfile(F):-
    seeing(S),see(F),
    readchar,readchar,readchar,
```

```
        readchar,readchar,readchar,
        readchar,readchar,readchar,
        readchar,readchar,readchar,
        readchar,
        seen,see(S).
  readchar:-get0(X),write(X),nl.
```

If 'end of file' and 'end of record' are represented as suggested in Chapter 5, the output from a call to **readfile** would be:

?- readfile('testa.txt').
97
98
99
100
101
10
102
103
104
105
106
10
-1
true.

If this is not the output produced on your system, it means that your version of Prolog uses a different way of representing end of file, end of record or both.

Question 4

It will be assumed that file in1.txt contains

first. second. third. fourth. 'fifth and last'. end.

and file in2.txt contains

```
alpha.
beta.
gamma.
omega.
end.
```

A possible definition of **combine** is as follows.

```
combine(In1,In2,Out):-
    seeing(S),telling(T),
    tell(Out),see(In1),copyfile,seen,
    see(In2),copyfile,seen,see(S),
    write(end),nl,told,telling(T).

copyfile:-read(N),process(N).

process(end).
process(N):-write(N),nl,copyfile.
```

Testing this by

?- combine('in1.txt','in2.txt','out.txt').

produces the output file out.txt given below.

```
first
second
third
fourth
fifth and last
alpha
beta
gamma
omega
end
```

Question 5

It will be assumed that the file test1.txt contains

```
first.
second.
third.
fourth.
end.
```

and file test2.txt contains

```
first.
xxxx.
third.
fourthxxx.
end.
```

A possible definition of **compare** is:

```
compare(File1,File2):-
      seeing(S),compfile(File1,File2),
      see(File1),seen, see(File2),seen,see(S).
compfile(File1,File2):-
      see(File1),read(X),see(File2),read(Y),
      comp(X,Y),process(X,Y,File1,File2).
comp(A,A):-write(A),write(' is the same as '),
      write(A),nl.
comp(A,B):-write(A),write(' is different from '),
      write(B),nl.
process(end,end,_,_).
process(_,_,File1,File2):-compfile(File1,File2).
```

?- compare('test1.txt','test2.txt').
first is the same as first
second is different from xxxx
third is the same as third
fourth is different from fourthxxx
end is the same as end
true.

Practical Exercise 6

Question 1

A possible definition using recursion is given below:

```
outsquare(N1,N2):-N1>N2.
outsquare(N1,N2):-
      write(N1),write(' squared is '),Square is N1*N1,
      write(Square),nl,M is N1+1,outsquare(M,N2).
```

?- outsquare(6,12).
6 squared is 36
7 squared is 49
8 squared is 64
9 squared is 81
10 squared is 100
11 squared is 121
12 squared is 144
true.

Question 2

The following definition uses the **repeat** predicate:

```
go:-repeat,get0(X),getrest(X).
getrest(10):-nl./* newline */
getrest(63):-nl,repeat,get0(X),X=:=10.
getrest(X):-put(X),fail.
```

?- go.
: abcdef
abcdef
true.

?- go.
: abcde?wxyz
abcde
true.

Question 3

The following program uses backtracking with failure:

```
find:-
      person(_,_,Age,_,Prof),Age>40,
      write('Profession is '),write(Prof),nl,fail.
find.
person(john,smith,45,london,doctor).
person(martin,williams,33,birmingham,teacher).
person(henry,smith,26,manchester,plumber).
person(jane,wilson,62,london,teacher).
person(mary,smith,29,glasgow,surveyor).
```

?- find.
Profession is doctor
Profession is teacher
true.

Practical Exercise 7

Question 1

The corrected version is as follows.

```
factorial(1,1):-!.
factorial(N,Nfact):-N1 is N-1,
     factorial(N1,Nfact1),Nfact is N*Nfact1.
```

?- factorial(6,N).
N = 720

?- factorial(7,M).
M = 5040

Question 2

A possible completed program is given below. It uses the same method of testing whether a number is even that was used in Chapter 4, i.e. use // to divide the number by 2, discarding any remainder, then multiply by 2 and check if the result is the original number.

```
go:-repeat,read_and_check(N,Type),
      write(N),write(' is '),write(Type),nl,N=:=100,!.
read_and_check(N,Type):-
      write('Enter next number: '),read(N),
      check(N,Type).
check(N,even):-N1 is N//2,N2 is 2*N1,N2=:=N,!.
check(N,odd).
```

Practical Exercise 8

Question 1

A possible answer is given below. Predicate **process** adds a fact to the database only if is not already there.

```
add_data:-
      assert(animal(dummy)),
      repeat,write('Enter next name: '),
      read(X),process(X),X=end,
      retract(animal(dummy)).
process(end):-!.
process(X):-animal(X),write('Duplicate entry'),nl,!.
process(X):-assert(animal(X)),!.
```

Question 2

The **display_animals** predicate defined below uses backtracking with failure to list the names of all the animals in the database.

```
display_animals:-animal(X),write(X),nl,fail.
display_animals.
```

Question 3

The **remove** predicate removes clauses from the database if they are present. If they are not, it does nothing but still succeeds.

```
remove2:-remove(dog),remove(cat).
remove(X):-retract(animal(X)).
remove(X).
```

Practical Exercise 9

Specimen solutions are given below. All the definitions require just one or two clauses.

Question 1

```
pred1([A|L],L).
```

Question 2

```
inc([],[]).
inc([A|L],[A1|L1]):-A1 is A+1,inc(L,L1).
```

Question 3

```
palindrome(A):-reverse(A,A).
```

Question 4

```
putfirst(A,L,[A|L]).
```

Question 5

```
putlast(A,L,L1):-append(L,[A],L1).
```

Question 6

```
pred2(L1,L):-findall([A],member(A,L1),L).
pred3(L1,L):-findall(pred(A,A),member(A,L1),L).
pred4(L1,L):-findall([element,A],member(A,L1),L).
```

Practical Exercise 10

Specimen solutions are given below.

Question 1

```
spalindrome(S):-name(S,L),reverse(L,L).
```

Question 2

```
remove_final(S,S1):-
    name(S,L),reverse(L,L1),
    removespaces(L1,L2),reverse(L2,L3),
    name(S1,L3).
removespaces([],[]):-!.
removespaces([32|L],L1):-removespaces(L,L1),!.
removespaces(L,L).
```

Question 3

```
replace(S1,S2):-name(S1,L1),rep(L1,L2),name(S2,L2).
rep([_|L],[63|L]).
```

Practical Exercise 11

Question 1

One solution is to place the operator definitions

```
?-op(200,fx,head).
?-op(200,fx,tail).
```

near the beginning of the program file and the clauses

```
H iss head [H|T]:-!.
T iss tail [H|T]:-!.
```

anywhere amongst the clauses defining the **iss** predicate (as long as it is before the final clause).

Question 2

Using the *univ* operator this predicate can be defined with just one clause.

```
addArg(Term1,NewArg,Term2):-
Term1=..L,append(L,[NewArg],L2),
Term2=..L2.
```

The original term is converted to a list, the extra term is added to the end of the list using the **append/3** predicate and the resulting list is converted back to a term.

?- addArg(person(john,smith,25),london,T).
T = person(john,smith,25,london)

?- addArg(city(paris,france),[a,b,c],T).
T = city(paris,france,[a,b,c])

The definition also works if the first argument is an atom, not a compound term. A term with one argument is created.

?- addArg(height,200,T).
T = height(200)

Practical Exercise 12

We can change the final two clauses of **sentence** to:

```
sentence([s3,both,V,NP1,Noun1])-->noun_phrase
  (NP1,_,Noun1),
  verb(both,V),adverb,{assertz(wordlist(verb,both,V))}.
sentence([s4,Plurality,V,NP1,Noun1])
-->noun_phrase(NP1,Plurality,Noun1),
    verb(Plurality,V),adverb,
    {assertz(wordlist(verb,Plurality,V))}.
```

and add a definition for *adverb*:

```
adverb-->[X},{member(X,[well,badly,slowly,quickly])}.
```

?- phrase(sentence(S),[the,small,men,sat,slowly]).
S = [s3, both, sat, np1, men] .

?- **phrase(sentence(S),[the,small,men,saw,slowly,the,dog]).**
false.

?- **phrase(sentence(S),[the,boy,will_see,quickly]).**
S = [s3, both, will_see, np2, boy] .

Practical Exercise 13

We can do this by placing a new predicate **lastnum/1** in the database to hold the
number of the last question asked (initially zero). When a new question is asked the
number is increased by one and this new value replaces the one previously stored.
To implement this we change the definition of predicate **runquiz** to:

```
runquiz:-
    retractall(myscore(_,_)),assertz(myscore(0,0)),
    retractall(lastnum(_)),assertz(lastnum(0)),
    title(T),write(T),nl,nl,
    askq.
```

and change the first clause of **askq** to

```
askq:-question(Qtext,Anslist,Maxscore),
    retract(lastnum(Last)),Qnum is Last+1,
    assertz(lastnum(Qnum)),
    write('Question '),write(Qnum),write('. '),
    write(Qtext),nl,
    write('Possible answers are '),genanswers(Anslist),
    requestanswer(Anslist,Maxscore),fail.
```

?-**runquiz.**
Are you a genius? Answer our quiz and find out!

Question 1. What is the name of this planet?
Possible answers are Earth, The Moon, and John
Enter your answer
|: Earth
You have scored 20 points out of a possible 20

Question 2. What is the capital of Great Britain?
Possible answers are America, Paris, London, and Moscow
Enter your answer
|: London
You have scored 50 points out of a possible 50

Question 3. In which country will you find the Sydney Opera House?
Possible answers are London, Toronto, The Moon, Australia, and Germany
Enter your answer
|: Australia
You have scored 10 points out of a possible 10

Your total score is 80 points out of a possible 80
You are a genius!

true.

Appendix 4
Glossary

Words in **bold** are cross-references to other entries in the glossary.

Anonymous Variable See **Variable**

Argument See **Term**

Arithmetic Expression A valid combination of numbers, **variables, arithmetic operators** and **arithmetic functions,** for example 4.37+6*X−Y+sqrt(67.4).

Arithmetic Function A **predicate** such as *sin*, *sqrt* or *abs* used in an **arithmetic expression** that (unlike predicates used elsewhere in Prolog) returns a numerical value.

Arithmetic Operator An **operator** such as + − * / used in an **arithmetic expression** that (unlike operators used elsewhere in Prolog) returns a numerical value.

Arity See **Term**

ASCII Value of a Character An integer from 0 to 255 associated with each of the (up to) 256 possible characters that may be used by the Prolog system. See Chapter 5 (Section 5.4) for a table giving the ASCII values of the most common characters.

Atom A non-numeric constant, e.g. *dog* or '*a long atom*'

Backtracking The process of going back to a previous goal to find alternative ways of satisfying it (see Chapter 3). Backtracking can be prevented by using the **cut** predicate (see Chapter 7).

Backtracking with Failure A technique that can be used to search through all the clauses in the Prolog database or to find all possible ways of satisfying a goal (see Chapter 6).

Binary Predicate A **predicate** that has two arguments.

Binding a Variable The process of giving a value to a **variable.**

BIP Abbreviation for **Built-in Predicate**

Body of a Clause See **Clause**

M. Bramer, *Logic Programming with Prolog*, DOI 10.1007/978-1-4471-5487-7,
© Springer-Verlag London 2013

Body of a Rule See **Clause**

Bound Variable One that has been given a value.

Built-in Predicate (BIP) See **Predicate**

Call Term A **term** that is either an **atom** or a compound **term. Goals** entered by the user, heads of **clauses** and the components of bodies of **rules** are all of this form.

Character One of a set of symbols that can be represented in a computer. These can be letters, digits, spaces, punctuation marks etc. See also **ASCII Value of a Character** and **White Space Character**

Clause A Prolog program comprises a sequence of clauses. There are two types of clause: *facts* and *rules*.

(1) Facts are of the form

    head.

head is called the head of the clause. It may be an **atom** or a compound **term,** whose functor is any atom (except :-). Some examples of facts are:

    christmas.
    likes(john,mary).
    likes(X,prolog).
    dog(fido).

(2) Rules are of the form:

    head:-t$_i$,t$_2$, ..., t$_k$. (k>=1)

head is called the *head of the clause* (or the *head of the rule*).
It must be an **atom** or a compound **term,** whose functor is any atom (except :-).
:- is called the *neck of the clause* (or the '*neck operator*').
t$_1$,t$_2$, ..., t$_k$ is called the *body of the clause* (or the *body of the rule*). It consists of one or more **goals,** separated by commas.
The neck operator :- is read as 'if'. Commas are read as 'and'. Thus a rule can be read as '*head is true if t$_1$, t$_2$, ..., t$_k$ are all true*'.
Some examples of rules are:

    large_animal(X):-animal(X),large(X).
    grandparent(X,Y):-father(X,Z),parent(Z,Y).
    go:-write('hello world'),nl.

Closed World Assumption Any conclusion that cannot be proved to follow from the facts and rules in the database is false. There is no other information.

Compound Term See **Term**

Concatenating Lists Combining two **lists** to give a new list, the elements of which are those of the first list followed by those of the second list. For example, concatenating the lists *[a,b,c,d]* and *[1,2,3]* gives the list *[a,b,c,d,1,2,3]*.

Cons Character The vertical bar character | used to construct a **list** from its head and tail (see Chapter 9).

Current Input Stream   See **Files**

Current Output Stream   See **Files**

Cut   A special built-in predicate used to prevent backtracking (see Chapter 7).

Cut with failure   A technique used to specify exceptions to general rules (see Chapter 7).

Database   The Prolog database comprises a set of **clauses** (rules and facts) which constitute definitions for one or more **predicates.** Clauses are generally loaded into the database from a text file by entering a *consult* **directive** at the **system prompt** (see the built-in **predicate** *consult* described in Chapter 1). Clauses can also be added to the database as a **side effect** when a **goal** is evaluated (see the built-in predicates *asserta* and *assertz* described in Chapter 8).

Clauses placed in the database remain there until one of the following happens:

(a) One or more clauses are deleted as a side effect when a goal is evaluated (see the *retract* and *retractall* built-in predicates described in Chapter 8).

(b) Further clauses are loaded into the database from a text file (if these include one or more clauses for a predicate already stored in the database, all the previously stored clauses for that predicate are first automatically deleted).

(c) The user exits from the Prolog interpreter (all clauses are automatically deleted).

Declarative Interpretation of a Rule   Rules have both a *declarative* and a *procedural* interpretation. The declarative interpretation is that its head is satisfied if all the goals in its body are satisfied. With this reading, the order of the clauses defining a predicate and the order of the goals in the body of each rule are irrelevant. See also **Procedural Interpretation of a Rule.**

Declarative Program   A declarative program is one in which the order of the clauses defining each predicate and the order of the goals in the body of each rule do not affect the answers to a user query (including multiple answers produced by backtracking). This aim may be either fully or partly achieved. It is considered to be good Prolog programming practice to make programs declarative as far as possible (see Section 3.7).

Directive   A goal included in a Prolog program, prefixed by the system prompt characters (see Section 4.1).

Disjunction Operator   The disjunction operator**;/2** (written as a semicolon character) is used to represent 'or'. It is an infix operator that takes two arguments, both of which are goals. *Goal1;Goal2* succeeds if either *Goal1* or *Goal2* succeeds.

Dynamic Predicate   See **Predicate**

Empty List   See **List**

Equality Operator   An **operator** used for testing the equality of two **arithmetic expressions** or two **terms.**

Evaluate a Goal   Determine whether or not a **goal is satisfied.**

Existentially Quantified Variable   See **Variable**

Fact   A fact is a type of **clause.**

Files   The same facilities available for input and output from and to the **user's terminal** are available for input and output from and to files (e.g. on a hard disk or a CD-ROM).

Prolog takes all input from the *current input stream* and writes all output to the *current output stream*. The user may open and close *input streams* and *output streams* associated with any number of named files but there can only be one current input stream and one current output stream at any time.

Function   A relationship between a number of values, such as *6+4* or *sqrt(N)*, which evaluates to a number (or potentially some other kind of term), rather than to *true* or *false* as for predicates. Prolog does not make use of functions except in **arithmetic expressions** (see Chapter 4).

Functor   See **Term**

Goal   A component of a **query** entered by the user at the system prompt, such as *go, animal(X)* or *factorial(6,M)*, which either succeeds or fails. The head of a **clause** can be viewed as a goal with, in the case of a **rule,** the components of its body as subgoals. The components in the body of a rule are also known as goals. Wherever they appear, goals always take the form of **call terms.**

Head of a Clause   See **Clause**

Head of a List   See **List**

Head of a Rule   See **Clause**

Infix Operator   A predicate with two arguments written using a special notation where the functor is placed between its two arguments with no parentheses, e.g. **john likes mary.** See also **Operator.**

Input Stream   See **Files**

Lexical Scope of a Variable   If a variable, say *X*, appears in a **clause,** it is entirely different from any variable named *X* that may appear in another clause. This is expressed by saying that the lexical scope of a variable is the clause in which it appears.

List   A type of compound **term,** which is written not in the usual 'functor and argument' notation, but as an unlimited number of arguments (known as *list elements*) enclosed in square brackets and separated by commas, e.g. [dog,cat,fish,man].

An element of a list may be a term of any kind, including another list, e.g.
[x,y,mypred(a,b,c),[p,q,r],z]
[[john,28],[mary,56,teacher],robert,parent(victoria,albert),[a,B,[C,D,e],f],29]
A list with no elements is known as the empty list. It is written as [].
The first element of a non-empty list is called its head. The list remaining after the head is removed is called the tail of the original list.
For example the head of the list [x,y,mypred(a,b,c),[p,q,r],z] is the term x (an atom) and the tail is the list [y,mypred(a,b,c),[p,q,r],z].
The head of the list
[[john,28],[mary,56,teacher],robert,parent(victoria,albert),[a,B,[C,D,e],f],29]
is the term [john,28] (which is a list). The tail is the list
[[mary,56,teacher],robert,parent(victoria,albert),[a,B,[C,D,e],f],29].

List Element   See **List**

List Processing   Performing operations on the elements of one or more **lists.** See Chapter 9.

Logic Programming   A style of programming derived from research in the field of computational logic. It is most commonly embodied in the programming language Prolog (Programming in Logic). The clauses in a Prolog program have a close similarity to propositions in mathematical logic.

Looping   Evaluating a set of goals repeatedly either a fixed number of times or until a condition is met (see Chapter 6).

Neck of a Clause   See **Clause**

Neck Operator   See **Clause**

Operator   A predicate with two arguments can be converted to an *infix operator* in the interests of readability of programs. The functor is written between the two arguments, e.g. john likes mary instead of likes(john,mary). A predicate with one argument can be converted to either a *prefix operator* or a *postfix operator*. The functor is written either before (prefix) or after (postfix) the argument, e.g. isa_dog fred or fred isa_dog instead of isa_dog(fred).

Arithmetic Operator An operator such as $+$ - * / used in an **arithmetic expression** that (unlike operators used elsewhere in Prolog) returns a numerical value.

Equality Operator An operator used for testing the equality of two arithmetic expressions or two terms.

Relational Operator An operator used for comparing numerical values, such as $<$ denoting 'less than'.

Operator Precedence   A number (also called the *precedence value*) associated with an **operator** that determines the order in which operators will be applied when more than one is used in a term (see Chapter 4).

Output Stream   See **Files**

Postfix Operator   A predicate with one argument written using a special notation where the functor is placed after its argument with no parentheses, e.g. fred isa_dog. See also **Operator**.

Precedence Value   See **Operator Precedence**

Predicate   All the **clauses** in the Prolog database for which the head has the same combination of functor and arity comprise the definition of a predicate. Predicates are sometimes described using *functor and arity notation*, e.g. write/1.

Binary Predicate: a predicate that has two arguments
Built-in Predicate: a standard predicate defined by the Prolog system
Dynamic Predicate: one that may be modified (see Chapter 8)
Static Predicate: one that may not be modified (see Chapter 8)
Unary Predicate: a predicate that has one argument

Prefix Operator   A predicate with one argument written using a special notation where the functor is placed before its argument with no parentheses, e.g. **isa_dog fred.** See also **Operator**.

Procedural Interpretation of a Rule   Rules have both a *declarative* and a *procedural* interpretation. The procedural interpretation is that in order to satisfy its head each of the goals in its body should be satisfied in turn, working from left to right. With this reading, the order of the goals in the body of each rule and the order of the clauses defining a predicate are of great importance. See also **Declarative Interpretation of a Rule**.

Program   A Prolog program comprises the **clauses** (rules and facts) currently held in the Prolog **database.** Unlike most other programming languages there is no fixed way in which a program must be used. Entering a goal or a sequence of goals in response to the **system prompt** causes the Prolog interpreter to search through the clauses relevant to satisfying that goal or goals, as described in Chapter 4.

Prolog   A programming language embodying the ideas of **logic programming.**

Prompt   An abbreviated form of **System Prompt**

Query   A sequence of one or more goals entered by the user at the prompt. In this book the more explicit term 'sequence of goals' is generally used.

Re-evaluate a Goal   Determine whether or not a **goal** can be **resatisfied**.

Recursive Definition of a Predicate   One that uses the **predicate** itself, either directly or indirectly.

Relational Operator   An **operator** used for comparing values, such as < denoting 'less than'.

Resatisfy a Goal   Find another way of satisfying a **goal**, whilst **backtracking**.

Rule   A rule is a type of **clause**.

Satisfy a Goal   Prove that the goal follows from the facts and rules in the **database**. This usually involves binding one or more **variables** (see Chapter 3).

Sequence of Goals   A combination of **goals** joined together by commas, signifying 'and'. In order for the sequence of goals to succeed, all the individual goals must succeed.

Shell   A framework which can be used for constructing any one of a series of related applications (see Chapter 13).

Side Effect   An action taken by the Prolog system, such as writing a line of text or opening a file, whilst attempting to **satisfy a goal**.

Static Predicate   See **Predicate**

String   A collection of **characters** such as 'hello world'. An **atom** can be regarded as a string (see Chapter 10).

String Processing   Performing operations on the contents of one or more **strings** (see Chapter 10).

Subgoal   See **goal**.

Sublist   A **list** element that is itself a list.

System Prompt   A combination of **characters** (?- in this book) output by the Prolog system to indicate that it is ready for the user to enter a sequence of one or more **goals**.

Tail of a List   See **List**

Term The name given to the data objects in Prolog. A term can be an **atom**, a **variable**, a number, a compound term or a **list**. Some dialects of Prolog allow other possibilities, e.g. **strings**.

A *compound term* is a structured data type that consists of a *functor* followed by a sequence of one or more *arguments*, which are enclosed in brackets and separated by commas. The general form is: *functor($t_1,t_2, \ldots ,t_n$)* $n \geq 1$.

The functor must be an atom. Each argument must be a term (possibly a compound term). The number of arguments a compound term has is called its *arity*. A compound term can be thought of as representing a record structure. The functor represents the name of the record, while the arguments represent the record fields.

A *call term* is an atom or a compound term. The body of a rule consists of a sequence of call terms, separated by commas.

Unary Predicate A predicate that has one argument. See also **Predicate**

Unbound Variable One that does not have a value.

Unification A process of matching, generally involving **binding variables**, to make two **call terms** identical (see Chapter 3).

Universally Quantified Variable See **Variable**

Unresatisfiable Goal One that always fails when backtracking.

User's Terminal A generic term that normally refers to the user's keyboard (for input) and screen (for output). See also **Files**

Variable In a **query** a variable is a name used to stand for a **term** that is to be determined, e.g. variable *X* may stand for atom *dog*, the number 12.3, a compound term or a list. The meaning of a variable when used in a rule or fact is described in Chapter 2. See also **Lexical Scope of a Variable**

Unbound Variable: one that does not have a value.

Bound Variable: one that has been given a value. A bound variable may become unbound again and possibly then bound to a different value by the process of *backtracking*, described in Chapter 3.

Universally Quantified Variable: one that appears in the head of a clause, indicating that the corresponding fact or rule applies for all possible values of the variable.

Existentially Quantified Variable: One that appears in the body of a rule, but not in its head, signifying that 'there exists at least one value of the variable'.

Anonymous Variable: A variable used in a fact, rule or goal entered by the user when the value is unimportant (see Chapter 2).

White Space Character A non-printing character, such as space or tab. Formally, a character with an **ASCII value** less than or equal to 32.

Index

Page numbers in **bold** refer to definitions in the Glossary (Appendix 4). Page numbers in ***bold italic*** refer to definitions in the lists of Built-in Predicates and Built-in Operators (Appendices 1 and 2).